CLARK ATLANTA UNIVERSITY
CHARTING A BOLD NEW FUTURE

CLARK ATLANTA UNIVERSITY
CHARTING A BOLD NEW FUTURE

Thomas W. Cole, Jr.

authorHOUSE®

AuthorHouse™ LLC
1663 Liberty Drive
Bloomington, IN 47403
www.authorhouse.com
Phone: 1-800-839-8640

Photographs in this book provided courtesy of Curtis McDowell

Published by AuthorHouse   03/05/2014

ISBN: 978-1-4817-7915-9 (sc)
ISBN: 978-1-4817-7916-6 (hc)
ISBN: 978-1-4817-7917-3 (e)

Library of Congress Control Number: 2013913539

This book is printed on acid-free paper.

CONTENTS

FOREWORD

Historically Black Colleges and Universities (HBCUs) in the United States have played a unique role in the development of the world's growth and development. They have created a bridge between the Judeo-Christian values of Europe and the tradition of compassion and spiritual perspective of the African Diaspora. A century ago, Arnold Toynbee recognized the unique contributions the African heritage would make to influence the United States of America to higher levels of sensitivity to the deeper human values and expanded conscience. Clark Atlanta University has been at the center forging the spiritual and material into a global alliance for progress for more than a century. The consolidation of Clark College and Atlanta University which created the University continues progress of the development and fulfillment truly of the Global American dream for the 21st Century.

Efforts to combine any two entities were, to be sure, challenging. When the two entities happened to be African-American institutions of higher learning, the challenges might be comparable to the Labors of Hercules, especially when both institutions had proud traditions, illustrious histories, and rich legacies more than a hundred years old. The challenge posed in this undertaking was compounded by the fact that one institution, Atlanta University (1865), was uniquely a graduate school, while the other, Clark College (1869), was uniquely an undergraduate institution. The schools were neighbors, their campuses being neatly separated by James P. Brawley Drive. Both institutions also belonged to the Atlanta University Center (AUC), the largest consortium of African-American educational institutions in the world. Through the years Clark faculty members have taught classes at Atlanta University and vice versa. Moreover, students from Clark, as well as the other schools in the AUC, have taken classes at Atlanta University for either undergraduate or graduate credit. Each institution had its own board of trustees, its own alumni association, its own president, its own faculty, its own budget, its own library, its own school song, and its own school colors.

Clark Atlanta University: Charting A Bold New Future is the story of a group of concerned and committed individuals who came together from both institutions in 1988 to explore possibilities for consolidating the two schools. Questions arose regarding feasibility and practicality of such a combination; chief among those were: merger or consolidation; name of institution; makeup of board of trustees; accreditation issues; seamless faculty; library resources; budgetary issues; and alumni associations. Without a doubt, the most significant question to arise was, who would be at the helm of this new institution? The name that came to most minds was that of someone intimately familiar with the Atlanta University Center (AUC), someone who had collegial relations with faculty and administration at each of the AUC schools, someone who had served as chair of Atlanta University's Chemistry Department, and later as Provost, and who had just been appointed incoming president of Clark College. That person immersed in the strategic planning, meetings, and preparations for the new institution from the very beginning was none other than the first president of Clark Atlanta University and author of this book.

The growing university became the largest of the member institutions of the United Negro College Fund (UNCF), significantly increased its endowment, and experienced remarkable growth in enrollment, fund-raising, and conferring of both undergraduate and graduate degrees. In a few short years, Clark Atlanta University had built a reputation that was recognized on the national and international scene. All these accomplishments were due to the dedicated men and women who dared to bring to reality the vision of "A Bold New Future." This book documents the work of the many players who participated in the consolidation drama of the two parent institutions that became Clark Atlanta University and chronicles their efforts, challenges, and successes. This is a history that covers 25 years—a quarter of a century, spans a generation, and is built upon the histories of two distinguished and related institutions. This task had few models in history—perhaps no models from which to draw definitive procedures. In this historical description and analysis, we are given access to the reflections and perspectives of the author and most notable craftsman of the model that emerged.

Andrew J. Young
Former Ambassador to the United Nations
and Former Mayor of the City of Atlanta
Atlanta, Georgia

CLARK ATLANTA UNIVERSITY: CHARTING A BOLD NEW FUTURE

PREFACE

In the summer of 1987, I must have changed my mind a dozen times about the decision to leave West Virginia and return to Atlanta.

On the one hand, I told myself the right thing to do was to stay as Chancellor of the state university system of 14 public colleges and universities, where I had been serving as the permanent chancellor less than a year. It was a position of some influence in the state and one that I had begun to enjoy. My wife, Brenda, was well-settled and adjusted in her position as Deputy Attorney General for the State of West Virginia. Kelley, our daughter, had done well in high school and was completing her first year of college. During her high school years, she was an active member of the marching and jazz bands, and in her senior year had won top prize as majorette. Thomas III was also doing well in high school, including extracurricular activities as a member of the track and football teams. We had just purchased a house, we had dear friends all over the state and in state government, and the last thing on my mind was pulling up stakes so soon and returning to Atlanta.

The alternative was to return to Atlanta to help lead Clark College and Atlanta University through what would surely be a period of unprecedented change. I had spent 15 years at Atlanta

University and my family and I had many friends in Atlanta. A firm decision made one night to return was overruled by my emotions the following morning.

By mid-summer 1987, I had two conversations with Vernon Jordan, the first to contact me about the presidency of Clark College, and then lengthy conversations with Carl Ware, Chair of the Clark College Board, and Thomas Cordy, Chair of the Atlanta University Board. Their arguments about returning to Atlanta were consistent and compelling. In the end, I knew what I had to do.

"He feels called," said Sister Mary Jocum, a Roman Catholic nun, told her fellow members of the West Virginia Board of Regents. She understood the personal turmoil I was facing in August 1987. William Watson, Chair of the Board of Regents, one of my strongest supporters and a good friend, knew what I was feeling, too. "I and the entire board understand why you feel compelled to go," he said graciously.

I guess I did feel called—for several reasons. In 1987, several reports cited that in virtually all elements of American society, including health, education, income and employment, the progress of African Americans had stalled, despite more than two decades of equal opportunity and affirmative action. The higher education system was not producing African American graduates in significant numbers, especially at the graduate level. Without the productivity of the Historically Black Colleges and Universities (HBCUs), the number of African American graduates in the U. S. workforce would have been far worse.

In 1987, the seven academic institutions that comprised the Atlanta University Center (AUC), the largest consortium of HBCUs in the world, represented a special group of private institutions of higher education whose proximity enabled them to offer programs of study far greater than each could have provided individually. I felt called to return to that environment because I knew it well and the prospects were exciting that a new university created from a combination of two of them could be structured to respond better to the challenges of access, equality and diversity in higher education. I also knew that Atlanta University had serious financial challenges, and Clark College had limited potential for growth because of space constraints. It was landlocked by a public housing complex on the West, Spelman College on the South, and Atlanta University on the West and North. For both institutions, only a major structural change could improve their viability for the long term. The combination of the two institutions made sense.

Exchanging the title of chancellor of the West Virginia Board of Regents for that of president of Clark College may have seemed a professional and career step backwards to some. But behind the scenes, discussions were already under way that would change that perception and had the potential to reshape the landscape of American higher education for African Americans. If plans evolved beyond merely increasing collaboration between Atlanta University and Clark College and resulted in consolidation into one institution, the new university would be the only exclusively private, comprehensive historically black university in the Nation with academic programs from the freshman year to the doctorate. There was reason to be encouraged that the discussions would be fruitful. There were no guarantees, but there was abundant opportunity.

This book is the story of what happened as a result of that opportunity—how events, timing, relationships and people of goodwill converged at a particular moment in time to achieve a vision for Atlanta University and Clark College and for American higher education that many thought was not possible in the Atlanta University Center.

Atlanta University, one of the oldest of the HBCUs, began in 1865 in a boxcar. Its history is well-documented in *The Story of Atlanta University*, written in 1968 by Clarence A. Bacote, first professor appointed at the university. In 1929, it gave up undergraduate instruction to Spelman and Morehouse Colleges and became the graduate arm of what was first called the Atlanta University System. That name was soon changed to The Atlanta University Center.

Clark University, founded in 1869 in Southeast Atlanta by the United Methodist Church, became Clark College when the institution joined the Atlanta University Center in 1941. Its history is described in *The Clark College Legacy* written in 1979 by James. P. Brawley, Clark College president emeritus.

This book complements the histories written by Bacote and Brawley. It describes the formation and development of the consolidated institution from 1988 through 2002. It contains dates and information about some of the events that occurred following the presidencies and untimely deaths of Rufus E. Clement at Atlanta University and Vivian W. Henderson at Clark College. Their leadership, sacrifices, professional and personal contributions and those of their successors at both institutions helped frame the historical context that made it possible for the two institutions to consolidate in 1988, following a very short planning period that lasted only a few months. It is my hope that the book serves as a tribute to them.

This book also reflects my personal and professional experience and relationships of more than 30 years as a member of the faculty and the administration in the Atlanta University Center. It is based on interactions with numerous people during my early years at Atlanta University and later as President of Clark Atlanta University.

I am indebted to many individuals and sources for facts which helped provide continuity and perspective. One of the most critical factors in bringing about the consolidation was the convergence of the right timing and the right people who quickly grasped the vision and the opportunity that consolidation represented. The primary leadership came from the chairs of the Clark College and Atlanta University boards, Carl Ware and Thomas Cordy, respectively, and key trustees: Elridge McMillan, Lamond Godwin, Prentiss Yancey, Marvin Arrington, Lawrence Cowart, Alvin Moddelmog, Myrtle Davis and Cecil Alexander, all of whom supported the idea and participated in the due diligence process to assure that the consolidation was carried out with the best interests of both institutions in mind. Kofi Bota, Nathaniel Pollard and Dorcas Bowles from Atlanta University and Winfred Harris, Larry Earvin, Gloria James, Carson Lee, Roy Bolton and Doris Smith from Clark College also worked diligently, often behind the scenes, to help finalize the details of a consolidation process that could work. Harris, Earvin and James assumed several different administrative assignments over the course of my tenure as president. Patrice Perkins-Hooker from Hollowell and Arrington, the attorney for Clark College, and Michael Baskin, in-house counsel for Atlanta University, coordinated the legal work.

Carl Spight, a physicist, and Conrad Snowden, a social scientist, interrupted their professional careers for eighteen months beginning in March 1988 to come to Atlanta and help provide a balance to our academic team to actualize the vision for the new university. Carl served for a year as Acting Dean of the School of Arts and Sciences and as Special Assistant to the President, and Conrad was the first Provost of the new university. Vernon Crawford, also a physicist and trusted friend, colleague and Chancellor emeritus of the University System of Georgia and Pearlie Dove, a respected alumna and retired member of the Clark College faculty, combined their experiences to lead the university through a critical important planning process that led quickly to accreditation of the new institution.

The intervention of Vernon Jordan, a member of the Clark College board, and Barbara Hatton, an alumna and former member of the faculty at Atlanta University and in 1988, a program officer at the Ford Foundation, helped the university secure a $500 thousand grant from Ford. It was a major grant at that time and it was matched by a grant of equal size from the Mott Foundation, which financed a portion of the consolidation costs during the transitional year. This grant represented a paradigm shift in support from the Ford Foundation for HBCUs since the 1970s.

The dedicated faculties, staffs, and alumni, while fiercely loyal to their individual alma maters, supported the bold new venture that brought them together. The students were especially enthusiastic.

There are many, many individuals, too numerous to list here, who were contributors to the university's success at crucial times during the early years. I owe special thanks and gratitude to my wife, Brenda, and children, Kelley and Thomas III, who supported me during fourteen years of eighty-hour work weeks and horrendous travel schedules. Acknowledgments go to Cynthia Miller, who wrote some of the chapters and conducted numerous interviews for this book to help recapture the historic details of the consolidation from a third party perspective. Cindy is a journalist with more than 20 years of experience and service as a former editor with the *Atlanta Journal Constitution* helped provide a third-person perspective. I am also grateful to Lynn Kinney, Kelley Cole Graham and Brenda Cole, who provided editorial assistance during the last stages of the writing process. To Ambassador Andrew Young, who wrote the Foreword to the book and who has supported me since my early days at Atlanta University, I owe a special thank you. Also thanks to Hattie Bell, Christine Hall, Vivian Usher and Gwendolyn Sapp for clerical and administrative support, the AuthorHouse editorial staff, Earle Clowney and to others who read all or part of the manuscript.

I am especially indebted to David Luke III, Chairman Emeritus of the MeadWestvaco (MWV) Company, whose friendship and financial support were instrumental in providing for a gift of $1 million during the University's second national fund raising campaign initiated in 1998. I am also grateful to John Luke, Jr., Chairman and CEO of MWV and to Douglas Luke, a member of the MWV board who personally contributed to this gift. I was honored to serve as a member of the MWV board for almost 20 years. The gift was used to support the endowment of the Cole Research Center at $750,000; the balance for partial support to the Office of the President Emeritus for 4 years.

Thomas W. Cole Jr., President Emeritus
Clark Atlanta University
August 2013

Harkness Hall Administration Building

CHAPTER 1

A Triumphant Bow

The excitement was running everywhere through the cool November air as I walked toward Harkness Hall shortly before dawn. The campus looked anything but normal: a stage the size of a boxing ring had been set up in the middle of the quadrangle, and temporary grandstands that could seat about 1,000 spectators were in place. Television cables snaked over the grass. The university, with all the spunk, charm and hope of the five-year-old that it was, would soon be introduced to the nation on "Good Morning America."

As part of a Southern tour, the popular morning news show led by its stars of the day, Joan Lunden and Charles Gibson, had decided to broadcast from the Clark Atlanta Quadrangle on November 22, 1994. It was an honor to be selected over other sites in Atlanta the crew had considered during its preview of potential locations for the broadcast. We were eager to participate in the planning of the program with less than three weeks to work with the GMA staff on so many details. Getchel Caldwell, then Associate Vice President for Development, and the university staff, planned a nearly flawless event.

Part of Caldwell's task was to convince the GMA staff of the importance of including representation from all the Atlanta University Center (AUC) schools, along with as many other metro Atlanta higher education institutions as possible. We had made

1

collaboration a priority at Clark Atlanta, and we wanted that reflected in the broadcast. It was no easy task to ensure that all AUC institutions were represented on the stage that morning, but for us, doing so was a critical aspect of our negotiations with the show.

As I arrived on campus at five o'clock in the morning, students were already in place and spirits were high. From my office in Harkness Hall, I had a bird's eye view of the staging area and everything happening both on camera and off. I could see the program director giving instructions to the crew; the show breaking away to national news and returning to local news; the co-hosts moving from center stage sometimes together and sometimes separately to other parts of the campus to interview guests.

As president of the host institution, I was told I would be interviewed early in the program so that I could give an official welcome. I could not stop rehearsing my opening remarks over and over in my head; however, by the time I was told to take a seat on center stage, all of my Atlanta University Center colleagues had been interviewed. I welcomed Gibson and his show to Clark Atlanta anyway. And then, in what seemed to me to be a rather abrupt shift in topics, Gibson introduced the question of whether Historically Black Colleges and Universities (HBCUs) could provide quality education to the best and brightest African-American students. This moment in the broadcast was preceded by an extensive report on black colleges and universities and their place in society thirty years after the historic 1954 *Brown v. Board of Education* desegregation decision.

Gibson had opened the segment with what he called "an appropriate question for our location this morning: Are African-American students better served by separate colleges or by a more integrated educational setting?" What followed was a report on the status of black higher education. Current students, educators and famous alumni such as film director Spike Lee, a Morehouse graduate who studied in the mass communication program at Clark College in the 1970s, weighed in with their opinions on the pros and cons of HBCUs.

I did not see any of that until just before my interview and had not been advised of the inclusion of such a piece during the extensive preshow discussions we had with the "Good Morning America" staff prior to the day's broadcast, so I had no reason to prepare comments on the topic. Charles Gibson and I were now alone on the stage, and Joseph Perkins, a syndicated columnist from Los Angeles and a graduate of Howard University in Washington D. C., was connected to us by satellite. Perkins' comments surprised me.

He said, "The biggest difference between today and thirty years ago is that the best and brightest black students are going to majority (white) universities, much like the best and most talented black athletes go to majority universities."

After what seemed like an eternity of Perkins expressing this line of thinking, Gibson turned to me. "Dr. Cole, thirty years after desegregation, Do we need black colleges?" So much was racing through my head at that moment, but I didn't have to hesitate to know my answer.

"Yes, we do," I said, firmly. "We need them now, and we'll need them in the foreseeable future. When you just look at the simple statistic that historically black universities enroll just 20 percent of black undergraduates but produce 40 percent annually of all baccalaureate graduates and that HBCUs are the baccalaureate origin of more than 60 percent of African Americans who receive the doctorate degree, that speaks for itself."

Gibson turned back to Perkins and asked him, "What will you say if your son comes to you one day and wants to go to Morehouse or Clark Atlanta?"

Perkins answered, "I will let him know that the opportunities for him will be a little better if he goes to an elite school, an Ivy League school, but I will let him know that I think he can get a good education at a black school and a great education at a white school, as well."

Gibson turned to the camera to close the show. I was stunned by the whole segment and still stinging from Perkins' comment that the "best and brightest" students don't attend black colleges anymore.

But I knew the students sitting out there in front of me were proud of where they were, proud of their school, their classes, their grades. I knew their parents had worked hard to bring them to this point and to this distinguished place. I thought of all the people who had worked so hard in recent years and in years past to bring Clark College and Atlanta University together in a consolidation that yielded new vibrancy and ensured the commitment to excellence.

I interrupted Gibson's attempt to close the show.

"You have to let me respond to that," I said. "We have some of the best and brightest students here at Clark Atlanta and the Atlanta University Center." The students erupted with yells and applause. I had made my point, and I simply thanked Gibson and "Good Morning America," and the show ended.

For me, that exuberant applause could not have been more appropriate, because this was truly a shining moment in the life of Clark Atlanta University. It was a moment that capped more than 100 years of two great institutions fulfilling their noble purpose and then coming together to achieve ever greater goals. It was a moment that belonged not just to those present but to all who had believed in and worked for the good of both schools across their histories. Not all the days and years had been easy. Adversity had done its work of squeezing and shaping a new future, but all the more reason that Clark Atlanta University deserved to take a triumphant bow before a national TV audience.

Reference

Transcript of Telecast of Good Morning America, November 22, 1994

Thomas Cordy, Thomas Cole and Carl Ware after ribbon cutting for
CAU Consolidation

Chapter 2

Seeds of Challenge

A major part of the history of the consolidation of Clark College and Atlanta University that led to the formation of a single institution can be traced back to more than three decades earlier to the Supreme Court's landmark ruling in Brown v. Board of Education. The 1954 decision that reversed the separate but equal doctrine was enthusiastically received by leaders in black higher education as a major step in removing racial barriers. But what was clearly a moral victory worthy of celebration held the potential to strike a devastating blow to black colleges and universities. Most schools did not feel the full impact of the Brown decision until the late sixties. But, Atlanta University felt it almost immediately.

A 1955 ruling allowing lower courts to set the timetable for states to enforce the Brown ruling meant that it would be some time before anyone realized exactly how the decision would remake the education landscape. The principles of the ruling were not even applied to higher education until 1956!

Private, black colleges and universities began facing new problems, including a growing need to obtain student aid for a rising number of students from low-income families. By the mid-sixties these institutions also suffered when traditionally white colleges across the nation began enrolling increasing numbers of black students, especially those who excelled. In Atlanta, institutions such as Emory

University and Georgia Tech were developing national reputations that brought the need for faculty and student diversity. The change created new competition for HBCUs, and especially for Atlanta University.

Founded by the American Missionary Association with assistance from the Freedman's Aid Society, Atlanta University had been transformed into a graduate and professional school when The Atlanta University System was created in 1929, making it the nation's first graduate institution exclusively with a predominately African-American student body. As the graduate arm of what later was named the Atlanta University Center, it was possible for undergraduate students to take graduate courses while still undergraduate students on a purely exchange basis and have this recorded on their transcripts. Atlanta University was also responsible for providing lands and space that would facilitate the relocation of Morris Brown College and Clark University to the Center. Until the Brown decision in 1954, Atlanta University was the only institution of higher education in the South where African American students could obtain graduate degrees.

As the impact of the Brown decision began to take effect, it was inevitable that Atlanta University would find itself vying with the nation's most prestigious graduate schools for top students.

The President of Atlanta University at the time of the Brown decision was Rufus E. Clement, who led the institution for more than 30 years. He died unexpectedly in October 1967 while in New York preparing for a meeting of the Board of Trustees. He was replaced by a three-person leadership team until a new president could be selected. The team was composed of Thomas Jarrett, Paul Clifford, and G. Cletus Birchette. Thomas Jarrett, dean of the graduate school of arts and sciences, served as chair and was appointed President in 1968.

Jarrett joined the Atlanta University faculty in the Department of English in 1946 following his education at Knoxville College, Fisk University and the University of Chicago, where he received a doctorate in English. In his more than thirty-year association with the graduate school, he witnessed social change that spanned the beginning of the Cold War in the 1940s, the integration of education in the 1960s and the expansion of diversity initiatives in the 1970s.

Just as Jarrett was becoming settled in his new role as president, an official meeting of the Atlanta University Board in April 1969 became the focus of a group of students who threatened to disrupt business. The Board came back together the following day in a hastily called meeting aimed at responding to the students' demands. At that time, the AU Board was an interlocking board that contained some of the members from other AUC boards and the Presidents of Clark, Morehouse and Spelman Colleges. Members of the board assumed the meeting would be giving the students a forum to voice their complaints over relatively minor issues such as unpopular rules.

What happened that day was far more dramatic. Students chained the doors of the third floor of Harkness Hall and held the trustees captive in a nine-room administrative area for almost twenty-nine hours. As padlocks were being placed on the third floor entrances, several AUC students interrupted the meeting and read a letter to the board that laid out an agenda for the student-trustee negotiations that would ensue:

"The time for white control of black institutions is over. The current boards of Trustees are a result of white control, and so they must be abolished. The first step we have made is to rename the University Center after our beloved brother Martin Luther King Jr. This is now the Martin Luther King Jr. University Center. We are now moving to collect resignations from all board members so that the control of the Martin Luther King Jr. University will be in the black community where it belongs."

The Reverend Martin Luther King, Sr. was one of the trapped trustees in Harkness Hall. He was quick to distance himself from the students seeking to name the center for his son, who had been assassinated one year earlier. "The King family would not condone any such request forced under these circumstances," King said.

The lock-in received front page coverage in Atlanta newspapers when some student protests—some violent—gripped campuses around the country. On the day Atlanta University's trustees were freed, black students took over an administration building at Cornell University in Ithaca, N. Y., brandishing guns. Hunger strikes and other forms of protests were staged by students at the University of Chicago and at Northwestern University.

The real issue for the students centered on uniting the separate schools of the Atlanta University Center (AUC) to become one university, an idea that was already under consideration at the time by a panel of experts. The other student issues seem almost quaint today—better food service, coed visitation in dormitories and the freedom to check out any book or periodical at the university library. The students also wanted representation on the Board.

After almost two days, the lock-in ended when Trustees signed a paper agreeing to the demands of the student protester. At that time, I was a member of the AU faculty in the Department of Chemistry. My colleagues and I watched the entire development from my third floor office window in Merrill Hall located directly across the Harkness Hall quadrangle. The Trustees later attended a meeting of the general student body, where students voted not to accept the demands and gave the Board of Trustees a vote of confidence.

This incident of student unrest was just one of the challenges Jarrett's administration faced. In addition to the push to consolidate the Atlanta University Center institutions, federal support for graduate education had been reduced. Expenses were soaring, and revenues were not keeping pace. Despite all the hardships, academics at Atlanta University continued to thrive under Jarrett's leadership. Early in his administration, he arranged to deed the property on the Southeast Corner of Chestnut and Fair Streets (one of the four corners at that intersection that Atlanta University owned) to Clark College that would allow expansion of the campus to accommodate construction of McPheeters-Dennis Hall.

There were a number of young faculty as well as senior faculty who continue to serve or who were hired during this period to strengthen the academic offerings of the University. A number of academic programs were initiated, including a master's program in African-American Studies under the leadership of Richard Long, and

12   CLARK ATLANTA UNIVERSITY

doctoral programs in political science led by Mack Jones. Graduate offerings in the School of Education were expanded under the deanship of Huey Charlton, such as educational administration, special education, urban education and early childhood education and creation of a new department of Public Administration was developed under the leadership of James Jones. Lucy Grigsby (who went on to serve more than 60 years at the University), Richard Barksdale and David Dorsey anchored the Department of English; Ben Hudson and Earle Clowney (who took over for Grigsby as University Editor following her death) served in the Department of French, and Lafayette Frederick chaired the Department of Biology with the first doctoral program offered by the University. Harding Young had left a strong legacy with a large accredited program in Business Administration, Virginia Lacy Jones was the dean of the only accredited School of Library Science in the state of Georgia (Jones later became the first Director of the new Robert W. Woodruff Library) and Genevieve Hill gave leadership to the only accredited School of Social Work in Atlanta.

Jarrett strengthened the faculty. By the time he retired in 1977, 67 percent of the faculty had earned doctorate degrees, a noteworthy accomplishment among black educational institutions.

With this backdrop, Atlanta University found itself struggling through the decade, but finally welcoming in 1977 a new president who was armed with new ideas for meeting the mounting challenges. Cleveland Leon Dennard was familiar with Atlanta. In the sixties he had served as principal of Carver High School and then as a planner and chief architect for the Atlanta Area Technical School. A native of Sebring, Florida, he had graduated from Florida A&M

University and received a master of science degree from Colorado State University and a doctorate in education from the University of Tennessee. Following his Atlanta stint in the sixties, he was president of Washington Technical Institute from 1967 to 1976, when the school merged with two other Washington, D.C., institutions to form the University of the District of Columbia. One of the plazas on the campus bears his name.

Within months of assuming the presidency of Atlanta University, Dennard delivered a radical budget proposal to his Board of Trustees. He proposed a $9.07 million budget for 1978-79 that was expected to produce a $2.4 million deficit. The 1977-78 fiscal year's expenses had been $7.7 million.

Dennard had crafted the proposal with improvement in mind. In his first nine months on the job, he and his staff, including Cleon Arrington, Director of Research and Development, G. Cletus Birchette, business manager, and Prince Wilson, Vice President for Academic Affairs, had conducted a comprehensive review of Atlanta University. The review updated a thorough self-study that had been completed in 1973 by President Jarrett and his administration. The update identified three major problems: inadequate enrollment, an ineffective management structure and insufficient fund-raising.

The Board of Trustees of this period had an impressive roster that included Atlanta Mayor Maynard Jackson, Coca-Cola Company President Donald R. Keough and noted economist Andrew Brimmer, who was chair for a brief period. The trustees had become increasingly uncomfortable about the university's ongoing financial problems. The deficit budgets that had been approved for years had stirred considerable debate, but the board assumed that a financial turnaround would eventually take place.

The board gave Dennard approval of his initial budget request, and he was able to start his first fiscal year with grand hopes of higher enrollment, increased research dollars and a tighter management structure. He and his staff regarded five years of dipping into the endowment to cover operating costs as long enough and shared the goal of putting Atlanta University on the road to financial solvency.

While balancing what sometimes seemed to be competing priorities, Dennard tried to improve the university both academically and operationally. He attempted to raise faculty salaries to the level of the American Association of University Professors (AAUP) national average. The move was considered necessary to attract and retain the high-quality faculty that was critical to bring in research dollars. Yet even a modest salary increase in the 1979-80 budget increased the year's already hefty deficit.

What had been a troubling financial picture for Atlanta University became a crisis during Dennard's years. The words "financial exigency" surfaced in a board meeting in June 1982, and two months later the idea of merging with another Atlanta University Center school came up in a board discussion. Although no specifics were discussed, Clark College was mentioned as possibly "open to discussion of such a move." The long-standing practice of having the presidents of other center institutions serve on the Atlanta University board of trustees was discontinued, although increased cooperation from the individual schools was called on during this time because of joint projects and concerns.

In July 1978, Atlanta University was awarded a $2.8 million grant from the National Science Foundation to establish the first of its four regional resource centers for science and engineering in the United States and its territories. I coordinated the writing of the grant while serving as Chair of the Department of Chemistry. Once it was awarded, I became the project director. This was a very significant achievement, not only because of the size of the grant, but also because the university had won a major national competition for the award. It had involved a lot of hard work and cooperation from colleagues in the Atlanta University Center and colleagues from colleges and universities from five states in the Southeast and with the Atlanta Public Schools. The AUC Council of Presidents reviewed and approved the grant application before it was submitted on behalf of the entire Atlanta University Center. This grant brought me to Dennard's attention during the 1978-79 academic year. Later that year, he asked me to join his administration as provost and vice president for academic affairs.

Time and attention were often split between Dennard's role as the steward of Atlanta University and his duties as the liaison between the university and the other Atlanta University Center schools. The complicated relationships between these member schools were redefined during his administration largely because of the building of the Robert W. Woodruff Library and the establishment of the Morehouse School of Medicine. Both were impacted by decades-old agreements among the six member schools of the Atlanta University Center.

Because the creation of the Morehouse School of Medicine would bring another graduate institution into the mix of schools at the

Atlanta University Center, the move was prohibited by the Affiliation Agreement of 1929. That agreement among Atlanta University, Morehouse College and Spelman College gave Atlanta University exclusive rights to provide graduate and professional academic study within the AUC.

The idea of a medical school had been around for years. In 1971, Atlanta University hired a consultant to conduct a feasibility study on the establishment of a two-year medical school. The Atlanta University board determined that it was not financially feasible. But during a joint meeting in New York in November 1975, the executive committees of the Atlanta University and Morehouse College boards decided that Morehouse College could move forward with the medical school.

The Atlanta University board cleared the way for the medical program in August 1977 when it passed a resolution that effectively altered the 1929 agreement. Three years later, President Hugh Gloster and the Morehouse board initiated plans to sever the medical program from the college, establish it as a separate institution, the Morehouse School of Medicine, and request admission as the seventh member institution in the AUC.

Dennard and his staff spent many hours on the medical school and its impact on Atlanta University in areas ranging from fund-raising to curriculum and even electrical power usage. The Atlanta University power plant served not only the University, but Clark, Morehouse and Spelman colleges as well, yielding cost-savings compared to purchasing directly from Georgia Power Co. The savings had been a factor in the decision in 1941 to move Clark

University from its site in Southeast Atlanta to the location in the Atlanta University Center. Dennard also represented the university's interests in the creation of the Robert W. Woodruff Library, a multimillion-dollar research library that would serve all member schools. Funded by a $12 million gift from Atlanta philanthropist and Coca-Cola magnate Robert W. Woodruff and named for him, the library triggered high-level negotiations among leaders of the Atlanta University Center schools. Because Atlanta University's library was funded by the General Education Board in the early 1900s to serve all black colleges in Atlanta, the university's role had to be central in establishing the new library.

The Woodruff Library would replace all the individual libraries of the Atlanta University Center, including the Trevor Arnett Library at Atlanta University. Library collections in the institutions were to be transferred to the new library, with individual institutions retaining ownership of their respective materials. Any new acquisitions were to be owned by AUC, Inc.

But while Dennard worked through all the details of these exciting new projects, the financial burdens were taking their toll on Atlanta University. Instead of continuing the old pattern of handling budget shortfalls by taking money from the endowment, the Atlanta University board decided in 1978 to establish a $4 million line of credit at the Trust Company of Georgia. The board intended for the university to draw on the funds over a three-year period as necessary.

The new solution to the money crunch fell victim to the same old problems: continuing income shortfalls caused by stagnant enrollment, little to no effective fund-raising and research dollars that fell short of projections or never materialized at all. By July 1980, the line of credit was used up, and an emergency loan of an additional $300,000 had to be secured to cover expenses for the year.

The bank debt became yet another drain on the endowment. In November 1980, the board authorized a withdrawal of $5.1 million from the endowment to repay the loan and cover remaining operating expenses for the fiscal year.

By this time, board members were openly questioning Atlanta University's ability to survive, and calling for an immediate reduction in expenses. Trustee Dwight C. Minton, chairman of the Finance Committee and chairman emeritus of Church & Dwight Co., Inc., developer of the Arm & Hammer brand, boldly stated that the university would "cease to exist within a short period of time" if it did not "review all of its activities."

That sentiment was echoed by many, including then-board chairman Jonathan Smith. In 1981, Smith announced to the board his commitment to "devote any amount of time and energy required to fulfill the long-term dreams for this center." He also said he "was prepared as chairman to go about the liquidation of the university" but not prepared "to continue following the middle ground which could only lead to failure." Even so, financial troubles began to consume the University, and the faculty was in open revolt against Dennard.

In February 1982, I accepted an appointment to become president of West Virginia State College in Institute, West Virginia. In the fall of that year, Dennard announced his resignation and left office in June 1983. The university's problems remained, however, with no prospects of an easy solution.

References

Henry N. Drewery and Humphrey Doermann, *Stand and Prosper: Private Colleges and Their Students,* Princeton University Press, 2001.

"Locked-In Rebels to Confer with Trustees," *The Atlanta Journal,* April 19, 1969.

Atlanta University Board of Trustees Minutes, Jarrett Administration, Vol. 1968-1977.

"Blacks Take Over Building at Cornell," *The Atlanta Journal and Constitution,* April 20, 1969.

"The Atlanta University Bulletin," Series IV, Vol. 172.

The Atlanta University President's Report, June 1978.

Interview with Trustee Emeritus Myrtle Davis, January 22, 2004.

CHAPTER 3

Deficits Set Course

When Luther Williams assumed the presidency of Atlanta University in July 1984, financial problems seemed almost certain to play a defining role in his administration. An *Atlanta Journal-Constitution* article described the university Williams was inheriting as "battered by inflation, rising expenditures, federal cutbacks and decreasing philanthropy." In spite of the problems, the board, faculty and staff were optimistic that Williams could steer the university in the right direction. The first alumnus to hold Atlanta University's top job, he had been heavily recruited by board members after the resignation of President Dennard.

Williams' background and research emphasis were consistent with Dennard's legacy of pushing for faculty to be involved in research. A native of Sawyersville, Alabama, Williams had graduated *magna cum laude* from Miles College in Birmingham, and then enrolled at Atlanta University for graduate studies. He earned a doctorate from Purdue University.

After a postdoctoral appointment at Purdue, Williams returned to Atlanta University to serve on the faculty in the biology department during the 1967-68 academic year. He returned to Purdue after a year at Atlanta University. He stayed at Purdue for nine years, last four years as the assistant provost. He then went to Washington University in St. Louis and in 1983 he was named vice president of academic affairs at the University of Colorado. Shortly after he began the job, an offer came to return to Atlanta as president of Atlanta University.

Williams accepted the offer but insisted on fulfilling one year of his obligation in Colorado. Throughout that year, he traveled to Atlanta monthly, working primarily with the board of trustees and acting president, Kofi Bota, who also had served on the search committee that tapped Williams for the job. "We felt that he was our man," said Bota, which accounted for the committee's willingness to hold the presidency open for a year. The strong support Bota gave Williams in the beginning would eventually wane to the degree that Bota would be one of Williams' harshest critics.

The University's Vice President for Academic Affairs, Bota served as acting president from the time President Dennard's resignation was effective in December 1982 until Williams officially took office in July 1984. Bota and Williams worked closely during the 1983-84 academic year, consulting with each other on the decisions that had to be made in the administration of the university.

There were many major decisions to be made. The university had reached an impasse: the deficit was growing, and the endowment was dwindling. At the same June 1983 board of trustees meeting in which Williams was unanimously approved as the new president, the board continued its practice of authorizing university leaders to "borrow from endowment funds to cover shortfall in cash flow for July, August and September." Not everyone agreed with the funding solution. Maynard Jackson, mayor of Atlanta from 1974-82 and again from 1990-94, asked that the record of this meeting show that he was opposed to borrowing from the endowment.

Budget issues shaped nearly every day of Williams' administration. Within months of taking office, he oversaw a one-year campaign to raise $3 million, an infusion of money that could both balance the budget for fiscal year 1984-85 and provide the resources to jump-start the initiatives of the new administration. Within a year, plans for a $40 million fund-raising campaign were in the works. The fund-raising campaign produced some much needed cash, but not enough. In his first year, Williams dealt with a proposal to declare financial exigency and floated the idea of merging with an Atlanta University Center undergraduate school.

But money was not the only challenge Williams faced. He also inherited vacancies in a number of key positions. Vice Presidents were needed for development, and finance and budget. The university also lacked a director of alumni affairs, a position that was key to fund-raising efforts. The dean of the School of Business Administration had resigned, and the business school faced threats of probation and loss of accreditation. The Schools of Education and Social Work were without deans, and other critical staff and faculty positions were vacant.

"In my view, the University had lost its niche," Williams said in an interview in March 2005. "In the 1960s, it had a monopoly on talent that was no longer true in 1984. This was true of the student body and the faculty—its artificial advantage was no longer true."

While some of the moves were met with resistance, it had become clear to many people that the time had come for real change, and that meant making some harsh decisions about budgets and resources that prior administrations had not been able to make. At a meeting early in Williams' administration, board member Dwight C. M summed up the situation at the university saying, "The neeu ror retrenchment had been discussed during the latter years of the Jarrett administration and throughout the Dennard administration, and each time the board had decided 'the pain was too great.' "The point of no return had been reached, Minton said, and there were no longer resources that could be used to fund further deficits."

The university's finances were given a detailed examination during a February 1985 executive committee meeting at the president's house. The key problems were evident: Revenues had never come in to cover the budget figures the board had been shown over the past several years, and that had led to huge deficits.

The budget for academic year 1985-86 was under review at a board of trustees budget and finance committee meeting in New York that was attended by Williams. Describing a "tight, conservative, probably a worst case" budget, the committee discussed the "shock waves" budget reductions would likely set off across campus.

Approval of the budget would require up to $3.8 million in either cuts or new funding. Essentially, unrestricted expenditures would have to be cut by 36 percent in order to balance the budget. Williams sought the board's support from the beginning on the budget proposal, pointing out that "the managing of opinion and reaction in connection with reductions would be very important." At the same time, a staff reorganization plan was proposed, and Williams also sought review of this plan by the board's education policy and personnel committee.

But Williams soon found himself caught between an increasingly irate faculty and a concerned board that was issuing directives to decrease expenses, raise more money and get the budget balanced. By April 1985, a projected $3.5 million deficit threatened the jobs of twenty of Atlanta University's 124 professors. About ten other administrative jobs were to be eliminated. Programs, degrees and entire departments were under review as Williams sought ways to get spending under control.

Files from Williams' presidency contain numerous memos, position papers, legal opinions and legal threats protesting the numerous changes he and his administration proposed to rein in runaway spending. The challenges came from students, faculty, staff, alumni and representatives of professional organizations. A publicly circulated memo from the university's five deans blamed the administration for poor leadership, and various groups called for the ouster of Williams and Smith. Williams incurred only wrath for the belt-tightening and got virtually no credit for his many proposals aimed at increasing the university's revenues. Under his watch some fifty-two new, and, continued grant applications totaling $6.8 million were submitted in 1985-86. He proposed a for-profit commercial and retail venture that would bring in revenue for the school and improve the economic opportunities for the area surrounding the Atlanta University Center campuses.

Williams' presidency was turbulent almost from the moment he had been offered the job. Most of the remedies he attempted had been as hard to swallow as bitter medicine. Not only had he spent three years cutting budgets, reorganizing faculty and staff positions and streamlining operations, but he had also demanded more from the faculty. He increased workloads, required research and for one year instituted a contract provision that required faculty members to raise a percentage of their individual salaries through research contracts. He limited tenure and promotions and pushed to have the university's bylaws changed to allow for dismissal of tenured faculty if the school was in a dire financial situation, which it was.

"I don't regret the three years I spent there," said Williams, looking back on his presidency. "I like to do difficult things. Given the problems (the university) had, could I afford three years out of my career? The answer is yes. "But I was reasonably certain that this wasn't going to work out before I even went to Atlanta."

Despite the stress, acrimonious relationships and bad press, Williams said he resigned comfortable with three major achievements: A science and technology infrastructure was in place that could support a first-class graduate program; performance criteria had been established that would help maintain quality; but most important, the university had not collapsed financially under his watch.

"I never took any actions that I didn't know were going to help the university," Williams said. "My job was to make decisions about the university, and I did."

While Williams' troubles had been taking their toll at Atlanta University, Elias Blake Jr. was facing long-standing issues at Clark College. The way he saw it, some of the issues that surfaced during his ten-year presidency had begun about thirty-five years before he even took office.

Clark University had pulled up its roots and moved across town in 1941, joining the Atlanta University Center and becoming Clark College. Trading a beautiful, magnolia-lined campus for a landlocked, square block close to Atlanta University and Morehouse and Spelman Colleges had triggered a competition of sorts. Clark College professors and leaders began to compare the school to the other AUC institutions and to vigorously compete for prestige and students.

Many of the students who began their college education on the old campus and graduated at the new one, felt their school had been placed in the shadow of the other institutions. Some were bitter years later. By the mid-1970s, several of those students had become tenured professors at Clark, and they led a contingent that Blake felt challenged him most as he strived to lead the college.

Blake had followed a very dynamic and charismatic president, Vivian W. Henderson, who died in office at the age of fifty-two. His accomplishments during his ten-year presidency show the results of a president with tremendous energy and fund-raising skills. Under his leadership, the college was enormously successful in raising funds from both the private and federal sectors. According to Brawley, "Henderson led Clark through a decade of unprecedented expansion in the developing life of the college."

Henderson came to the presidency with impressive credentials and brought stature that greatly enhanced the college with wide contacts and influence, locally and at the national level. Not only was he recognized as an authority in his academic field of economics, he was also a national leader in higher education. Under his watch, the institution's budget was doubled, and he provided leadership in the development of such options as studies in public policy, mass communications, general science, pharmacy and the dual-degree program in engineering. During his tenure, WCLK 91.9 FM was licensed. The Clark College alumni were strong advocates during his administration as evidenced by their financial support to the Centennial Celebration in 1969 and the Capital Campaign that was launched in 1973. Following Henderson's untimely death, Charles Knight served briefly as Interim President.

Against this backdrop, Blake took Clark through a decade of change. Under his watch, programs in mass communication and business grew prominent, freshman programs were strengthened and a faculty governance program was developed. It was a time of unprecedented advances in technology, and Clark College established one of the first campus computer labs in the country. Blake also represented Clark College's interests in the complicated negotiations with other Atlanta University Center schools to create the joint Robert W. Woodruff Library.

Blake had come to Clark College in 1977 from the presidency of the Institute for Services to Education, a nonprofit corporation that worked to increase opportunities for blacks in higher education. His background also included seven years as an assistant professor of education at Howard University where he conducted research on attrition rates and performance patterns of students in remedial programs.

When Blake took office, only fourteen of the 115 faculty members were tenured, and all tenured professors were in the traditional social sciences, humanities and sciences. There were no tenured faculty at all in the business and mass communications departments, two areas Blake saw as critical to the college's future success.

"By the time I got to Clark in 1977-78, a majority of graduates were already in business and mass communications, but the funding was from outside sources," Blake said. "My job, as I saw it, was to move a very precarious financial structure for those new programs." Blake's keen interest in business and mass communications matched that of his predecessor. Both he and Henderson saw the success of these two programs as key to the survival of HBCUs. "Henderson had perceived this reality," Blake said. "He was an economist, and he had already figured it out. The business people have all the money; I (create) a business program, and then I can justify seeking their funds. You no longer go to ask for money to help the down-trodden, beleaguered black race, you go ask for money to fund the education of the blacks they need in their businesses."

Blake pushed the computer on all fronts. He established a state-of-the-art mass communications department and introduced computerization in all administrative departments. During his presidency, the tedious, manual handling of admissions records was eliminated, and in the early days of intranet systems, Clark College's administrative offices were networked. They were also linked to the mainframe computer of the Atlanta University Center.

In 1982, Clark College launched its first computer lab for faculty and students led by Man Sharma, and by the end of 1986, four labs with more than 100 computers were operating. Some 70 percent of faculty and 45 percent of the staff were trained to use computers for word processing, record-keeping, budget management, exam preparation and grading and instructional uses in the Departments of art, English, history, math and chemistry. The number of students using computers on campus grew from fewer than 50 in 1982 to 1,350 in 1986.

Blake's push to move Clark College ahead in technology was balanced by his back-to-basics attitude about students and student life at the college. During his administration, study halls were held in the dorms five nights a week, dress codes were implemented for some Sunday meals and freshmen abided by a curfew. Sunday church services were held on campus, and a religious life program was introduced into the curriculum. A writing-across-the-curriculum program was introduced, making written communication a priority during his years. Despite these accomplishments, Blake's memories of his time at Clark College were clouded by ongoing frustrations with members of both the faculty and the Board. He inherited some of the issues; some grew out of his agenda for the school.

Tight budgets and the lack of a faculty governance system contributed to his discord with the faculty. Problems arose over chain of communication between faculty and board members, tenure qualifications, size of classes and shifting of resources from the traditional liberal arts programs to other academic priorities.

In September 1986, the board decided it was time for a leadership change and requested Blake's resignation. The board cited low morale among faculty and lack of communication between Blake and members of the board and alumni. Blake submitted his resignation in November of that year and left office the following June. Winfred

Harris, professor of biology and a Clark College alumnus and former academic dean, was appointed interim president.

The departures of Blake and Williams at almost the same time proved key components to the prospects for closer collaborations between Clark College and Atlanta University, including the possibility of a merger.

References

The Atlanta Journal-Constitution, May 1, 1984.

Interview with Former President Luther Williams, November 20, 2004.

Interview with Clark Atlanta University Huggins Professor, Kofi Bota, February 13, 2004.

Minutes of Meeting of Board of Trustees, 1984-1987.

"AU students, faculty celebrating news of Williams' resignation," *The Atlanta Journal-Constitution*, June 27, 1987.

Interview with Former Clark College President, Elias Blake, May, 2005.

CHAPTER 4

Consolidation
Discussions Begin

It was 1986 and Tom Cordy had again been up since two o'clock in the morning, with all too familiar thoughts of mounting troubles at Atlanta University. As the new chairman of the University's Board of Trustees, Cordy had a clear view of where the historical institution was heading, and that view was keeping him up at night. It was time to face reality: the University could not meet payroll, and its future was in question. So it was with a sober attitude that he sat down with Luther Williams to negotiate the president's exit from Atlanta University.

No one doubted that Williams had stepped into a tough situation, but many observers found his actions over the years inadequate in the face of the dire circumstances facing the school. The university's financial problems had now been simmering beneath the surface for almost two decades. Deficits had plagued the administrations of Jarrett, Dennard and Williams and troubled the trustees who tried to rein them in through the years.

"Serving on Atlanta University's board had always been tough, because finances were always a problem," recalls Myrtle Davis, who began serving on the Board in 1979. Declining enrollment and inadequate fund-raising were only part of the problem. An insufficient grants management system and a reliance on too many reimbursable federal grants and contracts also played a role.

The Affiliation Agreement of 1929 which established Atlanta University as the graduate institution for the Atlanta University Center schools had run its course, and that threw fuel on the fire. Integration provided opportunities at other graduate schools. As other member schools grew in size and endowment, their emphasis on sending graduates to Atlanta University waned.

When Cordy joined the board in the fall of 1986, he found the financial condition of the university shocking. His friend and personal attorney Prentiss Yancey, who was serving as vice chairman of the Atlanta University board, had explained the problems to him, but Cordy didn't fully absorb the extent of the crisis prior to joining the board.

"I didn't understand the severity of the situation," Cordy said. "It's like someone tells you they're not feeling well; you don't automatically assume they have cancer." A reluctant addition to the board, Cordy replaced Jonathan Smith as chairman shortly after becoming a trustee.

Cordy had become active in the Atlanta business world in the early eighties. He owned his own company, AMC Mechanical and Construction Co. He served on the boards of Kimberly Clark, First Union bank, BellSouth, Cox Enterprises, Central Atlanta Progress and the Atlanta Symphony. He served as vice president of the Atlanta Area Council of Boy Scouts of America, president of the Atlanta Chapter of the Urban League, the Atlanta Business League and

Atlanta Convention and Visitor's Bureau and treasurer of the Atlanta Chamber of Commerce.

So when Yancey came to talk to him about joining the university's board, Cordy's answer was simple: "No, I'm too busy." But Yancey was persistent, even suggesting that as an alumnus of the university, Cordy had an obligation to serve. Atlanta University needed his businesslike approach and corporate knowledge to help get it back on track.

The University was not the same one Cordy remembered from his days there as a graduate student in economics in the 1960s. At that time Atlanta University had enjoyed the largest endowment of the Atlanta University Center schools. When he began looking over financial reports, he saw clearly that the university had eaten as far into its endowment as it could. The situation had become so grave that the University would not be able to make payroll through the end of the 1986-87 academic year.

"When I looked at the situation from a macro perspective, it became clear to me," Cordy said. "A private (graduate) school with limited endowment—it didn't make sense to operate independently long term. The wise thing to do would be to put it in combination with an undergraduate program that would be a feeder for the graduate program. The combination of the two should make a stronger entity than either one of the individual pieces standing alone. That's the way I looked at that." Cordy discussed the idea with Clark College board member, Carl Ware.

Cordy and Ware had first met in the 1960s when they were college students on Atlanta University Center campuses—Ware at Clark and Cordy at Morehouse. Their social circles occasionally intersected, but it wasn't until they were adults that their friendship fully developed. Their wives, Mary Ware and Wilma Cordy, were also friends. The couples lived only a few streets apart and worshipped together at Ben Hill United Methodist Church in South Atlanta. Cordy's company was located just across from Ware's office in the corporate headquarters of Coca-Cola, and the two sometimes met for lunch.

Ware, who was president of the Atlanta City Council in the seventies, had been chairman of the Clark College board of trustees since late 1984. He had already distinguished himself as an outstanding leader and problem-solver at Coca-Cola, where his notable work as USA special markets vice president led in 1982 to his promotion to urban affairs vice president. In that role, Ware had responsibility for Coke's domestic and international external affairs and philanthropic programs. The company established the Coca-Cola Foundation in 1984 to support education through scholarships and grants, and as urban affairs vice president, Ware headed the foundation. Ware is credited with being the principal architect of Coca-Cola's disinvestment from South Africa in 1986, a move that contributed to profound change for the people of that country and was hailed by the African National Congress as a "model" for other companies.

As Cordy began to fully absorb Atlanta University's financial picture and the scope of the work that lay before him, he was convinced the university needed an immediate infusion of funds.

"I saw that the trustees of Atlanta University had essentially voted a deficit budget for nine or 10 years in a row," Cordy said. "They had eroded the endowment of the university and used it for operating purposes, operating funds. No significant outside fund-raising had occurred, and there was loose control." He turned to Ware, first for an advance of Coca-Cola Foundation money that had already been earmarked for the university. The advance would ease the pressing, cash-flow crisis at least for the short-term. He also turned to Ware for counsel and support on what must come next for the institution.

Sitting in the executive dining room of the Coca-Cola building, these two powerful friends drew on what they knew best: Why not use a corporate model to save Atlanta University and make Clark College stronger in the process? In the minds of both men, it would be wrong not to attempt to change the course of history that seemed to be looming before them. How could you not take advantage of this unique set of circumstances and opportunities to do this?" said Ware. "To have walked away from it would have been a terrible dereliction of our duties and responsibilities as trustees of both institutions and guardians of a history and culture."

Neither Ware nor Cordy takes credit for the original idea of bringing Atlanta University and Clark College together. It was discussed at several settings and at different points in time by Atlanta University Trustees, but professor and provost Creigs Beverly is regarded as the first person to put forth the idea in writing. Clark College Trustee Marvin Arrington and President of the Atlanta City Council who went on to become a Fulton County Superior Court Judge, was among the early proponents of such a plan. But Ware and Cordy were the catalysts for making it happen. As the two men talked over lunch in the Coca-Cola executive dining room, the first steps of what needed to be done emerged. They talked about who should be brought in on future discussions.

"We wanted to make sure that we kept it very tight in terms of who knew what we were talking about," Ware remembers. "The last thing in the world you wanted to do was to have a meeting of both boards of trustees to sit around and speculate, and then you have a front page news story. As we talked about it at lunch, we talked about who should know, how many other people should be brought into the discussion, and importantly, how we should go about communicating what we were talking about to the other trustees. That's what the first meeting was about. Neither one of us ever thought it was a bad idea. From day one, it was a good idea."

By early 1987, the friendship of Cordy and Ware had taken on a new dimension—that of strong partners who could work together to achieve much needed change. The two friends put together a small team that brought the right combination of skills, talents and loyalties. It was a group with the right motives and a common agenda—to preserve the essence of Atlanta University and Clark College while positioning both historic institutions for the future.

The inner circle of Trustees that emerged included Myrtle Davis, secretary; Yancey, chairman of the finance committee for the Atlanta University board, and his Clark College counterpart, Lamond Godwin, a senior executive with American Express in New York and a Clark alumnus. The vice chairman of the Clark Trustees, Elridge McMillan, a Clark alumnus who had just completed a year as the chair of Georgia's Board of Regents, and Arrington, a Clark alumnus who was president of the Atlanta City Council at the time, would need to be involved. Cecil Alexander, an influential Atlanta architect who was serving on the Atlanta University Board of Trustees and had been a Clark College Trustee, would also be brought in on the talks.

Connections and relationships ran deep, making working together easy for this group. Godwin, Arrington and Ware attended Clark College together; Yancey and Cordy had known each other since they were teenagers. Ware and McMillan had served together on the Clark board for years. Arrington and Davis served together on the Atlanta City council. All knew each other professionally. "We did not have to get to know each other, and that was a huge, huge plus," said Ware.

The early meetings focused on a general assessment of the two institutions—financial and accreditation issues, endowments and faculty and program strengths. Meetings were informal and private, often held at Yancey's Buckhead home. "We wanted to keep this very tight and very confidential as long as we could without abridging our responsibilities to our trustees . . . to make sure we were not doing or saying anything, making any commitments, without their approval," Ware said. "That was a very delicate tightrope to walk."

For Cordy and Ware, pursuing a level of increased cooperation between Clark College and Atlanta University wasn't just an idea. It became a passion to which they were deeply committed. As their fervor grew, it became clear that discussions needed to move beyond the conversations at lunch and in the church pews to serious strategic planning. Because of the relationships that existed, there was no resistance to the idea, to the concept," said Cordy. "The only thing that remained when discussions surfaced was strategically how would you get it done? How would you pull it off?"

One of the keys to a successful merger was clearly finding a leader capable of marshalling two historical institutions through a period of uncertainty and change. The requirements were tough: This leader needed to be a person who had credibility with Atlanta University, Clark College, the United Methodist Church, Atlanta business leaders and the national higher education community. Credibility with leaders of the other Atlanta University Center schools would be a factor, too.

Publicly, a search committee was hard at work looking for a new president for Clark College. At Atlanta University, Dorcas Bowles left her position as dean of the School of Social Work to become acting president, but she was not a candidate for the presidency. Privately, the small leadership group was thinking bigger. To them, the search was not for a president of either school. The search was for the person who could lead Clark College and Atlanta University into a new, intertwined relationship.

No one expected such an ambitious plan to be easy, and there was much to be accomplished behind the scenes before the idea could be made public. Continuing a search for a Clark College president was a necessary step for two reasons: Not only did it buy time for leaders to work on the possible merger, but it also allowed for the possibility that if merger were unsuccessful, Clark College would still have a qualified leader.

Meanwhile Atlanta University was bypassing the search process for a new president. With the university's future so uncertain, Dorcas Bowles and Tom Cordy ran the day-to-day operation until they could determine where the consolidation discussions would lead.

The Clark College committee cast a wide net in its search for a president. Several sitting presidents were interviewed, with many of the meetings taking place in the Atlanta airport to avoid publicity. The search criteria went well beyond consideration of resumes.

"You are really concerned about the ethics, the morals and the background of a person," said Delores Aldridge, a member of the search committee and the Grace Towns Hamilton Professor of Sociology and African American Studies at Emory University in Atlanta. "Race wasn't the issue, but it was on the sideline, and so was religious affiliation. You don't put all this in the criteria, but it's all very important." Even the personal lives of candidates mattered. "For example, what kind of wife does a candidate have? What kind of first lady will she be? It's certainly not part of the guidelines, but it's there," recalled Aldridge.

The position that needed to be filled went beyond the presidency of Clark College as long as there was an expectation that putting the right person in that job would be a pivotal step in uniting Atlanta University and Clark College.

As the plans for a new future for the two institutions began to take shape, my own plans were about to change in a way I had not imagined. In May 1987, I awoke to a day that promised to be an especially long, but interesting one. A full schedule of official duties in my role as chancellor of the West Virginia Board of Regents would be capped off by a trip to Atlanta for a secretive meeting.

By early afternoon, I had shaken hands with many of the hundreds of new graduates who participated in West Virginia University's commencement and listened to the words of then Secretary of Transportation Elizabeth Dole, who delivered the commencement address. But instead of ending the day with the usual three-hour drive back to my home in Charleston, West Virginia, I drove two hours in the opposite direction to the Pittsburgh airport. This was a trip I didn't want to talk about, because I didn't want to have to explain it to anybody in West Virginia, yet. That's why I had decided to fly out of Pittsburgh, so I could avoid any chance of seeing someone I knew. More than anything else, I was flying to Atlanta to satisfy my curiosity.

Earlier in the spring, Vernon Jordan, a partner in the law firm Akin, Gump, Strauss, Hauer & Feld and then a member of the Clark College Board of Trustees, had contacted me on behalf of Clark College. He said the college was looking for a president, and the search committee wanted to talk to me. While that move did not fit my professional plan, there was something intriguing about the idea of returning to the city in which I had begun my career nearly 20 years earlier. But because the timing seemed wrong, I dismissed the idea initially.

After a second contact by Jordan, I agreed to travel to Atlanta to meet with the search committee, chaired by Godwin. Ware and McMillan were members of the committee along with Major Jones, a Methodist minister who was also president-dean of the

Gammon Theological Seminary and a Clark College Trustee. In a sense, the idea of a greater calling was propelling me through this day that included a 6 p.m. meeting with the search committee at the Ritz-Carlton in downtown Atlanta, a 10-p.m. flight back to Pittsburgh and a five-hour drive home to Charleston from there.

Ware said my name was first put forth by James P. Brawley, who was president emeritus of Clark College at the time, and had served as president from 1941 to 1965. When we were in search mode for a new president for Clark College," said Ware, "Dr. Brawley called me up one day and said, 'I want to talk to you. There is but one person who can do what you need to get done for Clark College and, if you do merge the two institutions, for the entire enterprise of the new university. That's Tom Cole. I doubt if you can get him, but, I tell you, that's who you need.'"

I was not surprised that my name emerged as a candidate for the presidency. There were so many ways that my background seemed to intersect with the history and mission of Clark College. Its nearly 100-year association with the United Methodist Church meant something to me, in part because of my father's years as president of Wiley College, a United Methodist-affiliated school founded in 1873. I was raised firmly entrenched in the traditions of the United Methodist Church. My experience as a university administrator— serving as president of West Virginia State College and then running the state's university system—had prepared me for the kind of challenges Clark was facing.

McMillan, who was a longtime member of the Clark College board, was president of the Atlanta-based Southern Education

Foundation, Inc., recalls the board's focus as it searched for the right candidate for the Clark position. "We were looking for someone different, someone who could really move Clark in a different direction. We were really looking for someone with a national reputation, someone who could put Clark on the right course. Tom emerged as that person."

And to the insiders exploring the idea of bringing Clark College and Atlanta University together, my background was considered a good fit for Atlanta University, too. "Essentially we agreed that if we were able to get Tom Cole to come in and be the president of Clark College, he would be the ideal person to lead the project on the merger and then lead the newly merged institution," Ware said. "That was a conscious decision."

Clark's pursuit was persistent, and I continued to be curious about the potential of this opportunity. While no one was talking officially about the idea of consolidating Atlanta University and Clark College, I knew the idea had been around before. It had been casually discussed while I was provost at Atlanta University, and the timing of vacancies in the office of president at both institutions provided an opportunity that had never existed before. In the early conversations, I pressed the Clark search committee on whether a merger or consolidation was in the works. While there were no guarantees, members of the committee confirmed that talks were in process. Cordy later offered the same assurance.

Conversations continued through the summer, with Godwin serving as the primary contact to give me details on the position and other information. But despite my curiosity, it was difficult to focus on what was happening in Atlanta. I was approaching my first anniversary as chancellor of the West Virginia Board of Regents and preparing for my second legislative session. As usual, political leaders in West Virginia were debating the number of medical schools and community colleges because of concerns that the state's population might be stretched to support them all. My time was spent preparing to justify my recommendation that the state should maintain three medical schools and five community colleges. I was also busy outlining my recommendations to state government leaders for budget requests. I kept my interest in the Atlanta position private, confiding only in my wife, children and our friends, Charles and Lucia Bacote James, who also lived in Charleston, West Virginia.

Lucia Bacote James was more than a little familiar with Atlanta University. Her father was Clarence Bacote, the first professor appointed to the Atlanta University faculty in 1931. He had been among those who brought my name before the search committee that was reviewing candidates for the presidency of West Virginia State College in the early 1980s. Lucia and Charles were among the first people we met in West Virginia, and we became close friends. These dear confidants understood why I would be drawn to a situation that might save Atlanta University.

I accepted the Clark College presidency in August 1987 on the condition that I could remain in West Virginia through the legislative session which ended in March 1988, and, should Clark College and Atlanta University eventually combine, I would be the president of the newly created institution. The second condition was a private, handshake agreement between Ware, Cordy and me. "We felt we had identified the right leader," Ware recalled. "We felt we had the right strategy. We felt, frankly, that God was on our side to bring these two institutions together."

References

Interview with Trustee Thomas Cordy, December 21, 2004.

Interview with Trustee Myrtle Davis, January 22, 2004.

Interview with Trustee Carl Ware, December 11, 2003.

Interview with Trustee Delores Aldridge, March 16, 2006.

Interview with Trustee Elridge McMillan, December 3, 2003.

Interview with Former First Lady, Brenda Cole, January 30, 2004.

Chapter 5

Consolidation Takes Shape

After I accepted the position as president of Clark College, planning for the consolidation became an integral part of the discussions. On September 3, 1987, Cordy, Godwin, Ware and I met privately in Atlanta to discuss all aspects of the consolidation that we could think of at that time. We shared the belief that creating a new university promised a better future to respond to the new paradigm in American Higher Education than merely working to enhance collaboration between the two institutions. We discussed the process for engaging the two boards and getting the necessary support from other key individuals and constituent groups. We discussed the vision we all shared about the new university.

The vision was framed against five major themes that the two institutions historically did best:

1. Increase the number at the bachelor's, master's and doctorate levels of outstanding graduates who will constitute a technologically sophisticated workforce that will increasingly be made up of members of ethnic minorities and women who will compete successfully in the global economy,

2. Increase the Nation's expertise in mathematics, science, and engineering by engaging in cutting-edge research,

3. Enhance the quality of the Nation's public schools with a particular emphasis on urban education,

4. Train a new cadre of entrepreneurs, librarians, social workers, and foreign service personnel, and

5. Provide community service and technical assistance to improve the quality of life for the larger society, both locally and abroad.

We talked about the importance of having discussions with representatives from the trustees, faculty, staff, alumni, students and key supporters, but agreed on the need to keep the number of persons involved at a minimum during the early stages. We discussed the timeline for a public announcement and the rationale for forming a joint board committee. This discussion was summarized in a two-page document that served as our operating plan for the period between that September meeting and my coming on board as president in March 1988.

My appointment was announced to the general public in an *Atlanta Journal-Constitution* article on September 9, 1987. Following separate meetings of the boards of both Atlanta University and Clark College, the idea of exploring greater collaboration between the two institutions was officially before the Trustees. A press conference and joint press release from Cordy and Ware announced that conversations about a possible merger between Clark College and Atlanta University were under way, and the news appeared in the local paper November 11, 1987.

Pieces were falling into place. The idea of combining the two institutions was moving forward. For the next six months, I traveled to Atlanta monthly from West Virginia to participate in discussions with Ware, Cordy and other Trustees. Both schools created study committees, with the expectation that these two independent committees would begin meeting together in January 1988.

Shortly before that, I sent Ware and Godwin a memorandum outlining the history of cooperation in the Atlanta University Center and summarizing the issues that should serve as a basis for discussion at that first meeting of the Joint Board_Committee, scheduled for January 20, 1988.

Elridge McMillan chaired the Clark study committee, and Prentiss Yancey chaired the Atlanta University counterpart. The two men became co-chairs of the Joint Board Committee when it was formed. But before the two groups had combined, the individual committees had met on several occasions to determine each school's priorities.

The first official meeting of the Clark committee took place November 20, 1987, at the Commerce Club, a private club in downtown Atlanta. Besides Ware and McMillan, other board members attending included the Reverend Cornelius Henderson, Marvin Arrington and Carson Lee. Board members A.D. Moddelmog and Lamond Godwin were also on the study committee, but not present at the first meeting. Attorneys Patrice Perkins-Hooker and Lou Horne from Arrington's law firm were also present.

The list of priorities for Clark that emerged from its first meeting included:

- Maintaining its relationship with the United Methodist Church
- Protecting the name Clark College and making sure the name would be dealt with at the very beginning of any joint discussions with Atlanta University

- Being clear that if a merger took place, a leader had already been selected
- Going into any joint meetings with Atlanta University with a strong plan of action

For Atlanta University, the issues were comparable, and there was a preference to retain the name of the city, Atlanta, somewhere in the name of the institution. At that time, Atlanta University was one of only a few private HBCUs that carried the name of the city in which it resided. "The delicate nature of what we had to do was to frame some of the issues and come up with some of the things we would expect to get out of this or some of the positions we think might be deal-breakers," said McMillan of those early meetings.

The group needed to determine "which things needed to get dealt with early on rather than later on . . . simple things—or what one would think would be simple things—like coming to terms with the name, colors, song for the alma mater, the mottos," McMillan said. "In many cases those were the easiest things to deal with. But as co-chair, I insisted that they be put on the table early on, instead of later on." The Atlanta University and Clark College study committees came together as one group January 20, 1988, at Yancey's office in the First Atlanta Tower. The Joint Board Committee was composed of the following:

Clark College	Atlanta University
Marvin A. Arrington, trustee	Cecil Alexander, trustee
Lamond Godwin, trustee	Charlotte Blount, trustee
Winfred Harris, acting president	Dorcas Bowles, acting president
Cornelius Henderson, trustee	Myrtle Davis, trustee
Carson Lee, faculty	Kofi Bota, faculty
Alvin Moddelmog, trustee	Harold Doley, trustee
Elridge McMillan, cochair	Prentiss Yancey, co-chair
Carl Ware, CC Board Chair	Thomas Cordy, AU Board Chair

Staff

Thomas W. Cole Jr., president-elect, Clark College

Doris Smith, recording secretary

Michael Baskin, general counsel, Atlanta University

Patrice Perkins-Hooker, legal advisor to Clark College

During the four months that followed, the joint committee studied and offered recommendations on the two institution's academic, financial, governance and accreditation issues; building and land ownership; relationships to the United Methodist Church, Atlanta University Center member schools, United Negro College Fund and other groups; and the name, colors, mascot, logo and motto of the new university that would be created. The committee also agreed to recruit a blue-ribbon panel of nationally known education leaders to serve as an advisory committee.

Very little time was spent among board members on the question of whether or not the two schools should combine. That was decided in principal by Cordy, Ware and the small group of insiders. Although members of either board had the right to challenge the idea, the unity of the board chairmen of both schools sent a strong signal of support for the idea. Attention by the Joint Board Committee from the start was on the question of how, not if, Clark College and Atlanta University would combine.

Detailed minutes were kept by Doris Smith from the series of meetings of the Joint Board Committee. The discussions that were carefully recounted in those minutes focused on a range of topics from the legal definitions of "consolidation" and "merger" to the use of outside consultants. But the minutes are much less specific when it comes to the issue of deciding the name of the new institution. Little more is recorded in the official minutes than the sentence, "A considerable discussion followed relative to the name of the new entity."

There was considerable discussion, indeed, and not all of it took place in the meeting room during that January meeting, when the name Clark Atlanta University was introduced. Representatives of both schools brought their agenda to the discussions. For most of the Clark representatives, it was important that the name "Clark" be first. For most of the Atlanta representatives, in and outside the room, keeping the words Atlanta and University together was important.

But to others, including the chairman of the Atlanta University Trustees, the name was insignificant. "I was not going to allow a name to derail an event of that significance and jeopardize the future of those two institutions," Cordy said. "My position was very simple: We're not going to allow the name to derail this effort. The severity of the situation was such that we were trying to keep the doors open." Committee members tried out different combinations of "Clark,"

"Atlanta" and "University." On the table was Atlanta University, Clark University, Atlanta Clark University, Clark University of Atlanta, the Corporation for Clark College and Atlanta University and, finally, Clark Atlanta University.

Several things were appealing about the name Clark Atlanta University. There was no hyphen to perpetuate the idea of two institutions; both names were included; the words Atlanta and University stayed intact; and the acronym CAU had a nice ring to it, as a later editorial in the *Atlanta Journal-Constitution* would point out.

"In relative terms, we talked about it a good deal," McMillan said. "Each person, and then each institution, had their reasons for why they were suggesting one name or another. It was not hastily done. There was ample discussion. I knew what I wanted the result to be—Clark Atlanta University—so I tried to direct the conversation away from that initially, and as I remember, Clark Atlanta University was the compromise name that all of us could agree on. It was like unanimous."

The committee next turned its attention to the myriad legal issues that would—or could—arise in the process of turning the two schools into one. Michael Baskin was general counsel for Atlanta University. Subsequently, He spent 16 years as general counsel for Clark Atlanta University. Patrice Perkins-Hooker, then a member of Clark trustee Marvin Arrington's law firm, led the legal team on behalf of Clark College. These attorneys were tasked with investigating the consolidation from a legal standpoint, starting with the basics. What legal form should this combination take?

There were few models to turn to in the world of higher education. This was not a case of one school shutting down and being taken over by another, but a proposed combination of schools with fairly equal standing. We reviewed the details of the background and circumstances surrounding the merger of Case Institute of Technology and Western Reserve University that created Case Western Reserve University. We also looked at the merger of Straight College and the University of New Orleans that produced Dillard University. We reviewed the formation of Huston-Tillotson College and the combination of Peabody College and Vanderbilt University in Nashville. George Peabody College for Teachers, with origins dating to 1785, was absorbed by Vanderbilt University in the summer of 1979 to become the Peabody College of Education and Human Development at Vanderbilt.

We read all we could find about the mergers of these institutions, and I spent a full day in Nashville meeting with Vanderbilt's Chancellor Emeritus Alexander Heard, President Joe Wyatt and other officials at the university. Heard had served as chancellor of Vanderbilt at the time of the merger with Peabody. I shared my observations in writing about that merger with Baskin, Hooker and the joint board committee.

The conversations I had in Nashville were very helpful and made it clear to me that a merger of Atlanta University and Clark College would not be the best approach to combining the two institutions. Initially, there had been a consensus that a merger would take place, but Baskin and Hooker confirmed from a legal standpoint that a consolidation would be preferred over merger. A merger involves the union of two corporations by transferring the assets and liabilities of one (the "merged" corporation) to the other (the "surviving" corporation, which continues to exist). The assets and liabilities of the merged corporation become the assets and liabilities of the surviving corporation. In a consolidation, a new corporation must be created. The assets and liabilities of the two consolidating corporations become the assets and liabilities of the new corporation. The two consolidating corporations go out of business. In either a merger or consolidation, the surviving or new corporation receives the assets, privileges, immunities and powers of each of the merged or consolidated corporations.

"Whether we were going to consolidate or whether we were going to merge was a strategic move," said Hooker. "With the consolidation, it kept egos down at the two institutions. No one was being consumed by the other. From a legal point of view, it allowed both boards to represent that they were forming a new entity that was being renamed and reflecting the strengths of each other." From my vantage point it wasn't a matter of egos, but of the legal ramifications of choosing a merger or consolidation. There were previous agreements to consider between Atlanta University, Morehouse College and Spelman College. The Affiliation Agreement of 1929 cast Atlanta University as the graduate arm of all Atlanta University Center schools. Other agreements appeared to give Morehouse and Spelman partial ownership rights to a main building on Atlanta University's campus—Harkness Hall.

The Joint Board Committee needed to know what to expect once the consolidation of the schools approached reality. Doing the legal homework was critical to avoid complications with the sister institutions in the AUC. For Baskin, investigation involved a three-day trip to New York to dig for the original documents that formed the basis of arrangements between Atlanta University, Morehouse and Spelman. Many of Atlanta University's historical documents are housed in the Rockefeller Center archives, because the philanthropist was a strong supporter of the university. Baskin combed through original drafts of agreements, letters between presidents, board minutes and other notes to determine the intent of the deals that had been made in the past.

Baskin, Bowles and I anticipated conflict over Harkness Hall, the main administrative building shared by the university and Morehouse and Spelman colleges. Atlanta University occupied most of the third floor, and Morehouse used most of the second and half of the first floor. The building had been shared since its construction in 1931, and understanding of its true ownership had blurred with the passing of years. Due diligence uncovered historical evidence that confirmed Atlanta University's ownership of the building. However, if Atlanta University was merged into Clark College, that ownership could still become an issue.

"Had we merged the institutions, certain agreements, certain entities would have been extinguished," Baskin said. "And had they been extinguished, some of the language in some of the agreements would have triggered other things." For example, had Atlanta University merged into Clark College, a case might be made that Morehouse and Spelman had no agreement with Clark, and therefore had a right to Harkness Hall that the college couldn't claim. This could be true if a merger took place because, legally, it could be seen that Atlanta University had ceased to exist, and Clark College had assumed the legal rights of the university. And Morehouse and Spelman had no agreements with Clark College.

"To me, Hooker said, it was a very complex thing to do because of the myriad of issues we had to deal with. Even to come to consolidation as an option, we had to go through all of the agreements, find out what we could do, what could come back as ramifications. I think that any time you combine in any format two on-going entities with long histories and a lot of contractual relationships, that in itself is difficult. But it makes it complex when those two entities with their own individual lives have a special, unique blend with five other folks."

Committee work moved along quickly during the first few months of 1988. Subcommittees were formed on topics ranging from financial status to academics. The Joint Board Committee was not expected to resolve every issue and hand over to the full boards a completed plan for consolidation. The goal was to determine whether a combination of the two institutions made sense, outline a timetable and action plan and anticipate problems. Many final decisions would involve research and expertise beyond the study committee, and take more time than the group's self-imposed, six-month deadline.

Meetings were kept quiet and behind the scenes. The usual rumors circulated around the campuses, but there were no leaks of details or interviews with the Atlanta newspapers. This behind-the-scenes collaboration should be attributed to how well the Joint Board Committee members worked together. Members of the committee recall virtually all meetings being productive, civil and respectful. The leadership of Cordy and Ware is consistently cited as key to the success of the ongoing discussion.

"Tom Cordy and Carl Ware really took the lead in initiating most of the efforts, carrying this to completion," said Myrtle Davis, secretary of the Atlanta University board of trustees during this time. Ware and Cordy trusted each other, and trusted themselves to provide steady joint leadership. "Tom (Cordy) and I made a pact: We would always be together publicly," said Ware. "We could disagree and agree to disagree privately, but when we came out on an issue, Tom Cordy and I would be as one. "That was the pact that we made. That, I believe, was the key to leadership and the eventual smoothness by which this merger took place."

The timetable called for a Consolidation Agreement to go before the two boards by late May 1988, followed by a vote by the individual boards in June. The new institution would be incorporated on July 1, 1988. The year that followed would be considered the "transition year" for both Atlanta University and Clark College, and the new Clark Atlanta University would operate all facets of the combined institutions beginning July 1, 1989.

The consolidation of the two schools would create a new institution that offered 37 degree programs to a student population of 2,950 with 183 full-time faculty. For the 1987-88 academic year, Clark College's operating budget was $17 million with a $4.2 million endowment; Atlanta University's budget was $20 million, and its endowment was $11 million.

By April, the Joint Board Committee was ready to present its plan to the full boards of both Atlanta University and Clark College. The task of writing the final report fell to me as president of Clark College and prospective president of the new institution. I invited Winfred Harris, Dorcas Bowles and Kofi Bota, members of the Joint Board Committee who were familiar with the deliberations, to assist and make sure we dotted as many "Is" and crossed as many "Ts" as possible.

The final report of the Joint Board Committee provided the first comprehensive look at the idea of consolidating the two institutions. It was to sum up months of study by the committee and include data, research and recommendations to the full boards. We hoped the report would serve as a charter for the new Clark Atlanta University.

I dashed off a quick first draft that I typed myself to limit the number of people who saw it. The draft then went back and forth among Harris, Bota, Bowles, and me, as we worked after hours and behind the scenes, sometimes through the night. This document, dated April 19, 1988, would also serve as a starting point for the Consolidation Advisory Committee, a team of outside education experts selected by the Joint Board Committee that would submit its own report two months later.

The final version of the Joint Board Committee document included a vision statement and guiding philosophy, as well as summaries of academic and faculty considerations. It explained the difference between consolidation and merger, recommended a proposed administrative organization and suggested the structure of a new board of trustees. It also named the new institution Clark

Atlanta University. Throughout the document, especially in areas concerning faculty and staff, we were careful to use wording such as "one possible scenario could be . . ." to indicate that the summary contained recommendations, not decisions.

This was especially true in the area of academics. The document provided great detail on how the Joint Board Committee members saw the academic programs of the two schools best combined. It recommended changes that would bring more than $700,000 a year in savings, primarily through the combination of graduate and undergraduate programs and the elimination of some faculty positions. While much time went into crafting such a plan, many of the suggestions would be revised and refined after faculty input during the transition year. Since preparation of the document occurred in the early days of word processing, we pulled in Carol Johnson, a member of Bota's staff, to polish the report with headings, boldface type and other simple visual enhancements.

As Johnson typed the final version of the report, she remembered a letter Bota had received from a former Atlanta University professor. In this letter, the professor stated that the new university must chart a bold new future. So she named the document "Charting a Bold New Future."

Governance of this new university was discussed at many of the Joint Board Committee meetings. At the time of these discussions, Clark College had a board of trustees made up of 34 members; Atlanta University's had 17 members and five vacant seats. The committee put forth several scenarios for creating a new board, including the idea of creating a third, joint board that would operate over the two existing boards for a six-month period, and then replace the existing boards.

Other elaborate ideas were considered, but ultimately both boards simply came together as one on July 1, 1988. The incorporation document states that the board would consist of 40 members, 20 from each school, including two students and two members from the faculty. The issue of board membership was resolved surprisingly easily. Several trustees on both original boards offered to step aside so that the final composition would represent an equal number of representatives from both the Clark College and Atlanta University boards. Cordy and Ware served as joint board chairs, an arrangement that lasted for one year.

Also debated at nearly every meeting of the Joint Board Committee was the question of using outside consultants. Were they needed? At first, the committee remained split on the idea. Some saw the expertise on the boards, faculty and staff of the two schools as enough, and felt that keeping the discussions inside was most appropriate. Others saw a need for outside help ranging from planning experts to CPAs.

Winfred Harris, a member of the Joint Board Committee and most recently acting president of Clark College, put forth the compromise: lay the groundwork in-house, and then seek expert opinions. The committee would solicit a team of highly respected education experts to review the consolidation plan, comment on it and make recommendations for the transition. More than anything else, this panel would bring legitimacy to the process, and validate the months of work by the Joint Board Committee.

By April 1988, this expert panel began to take shape. Seven experts were selected from a long list of distinguished educators. According to Ware's charge to the panel at the April committee meeting, this group would bring "intellectual integrity" to the issue of consolidation and help the committee, the new board and the new administration sort out the issues. Ware maintained that the committee needed the experts' "credibility and clout" so that the new venture would be regarded as having had some of the "best expertise" involved in its consolidation process.

There was no doubt that each and every member of this panel, known as the Consolidation Advisory Committee, had credibility, starting with its chairman, Vernon Crawford, chancellor emeritus of the Georgia Board of Regents. This was the first of two major advisory roles Crawford would play in the consolidation. Other members of the Consolidation Advisory Committee were:

Robert H. Atwell, president of the American Council on Education.

Lisle C. Carter Jr., general counsel for United Way of America, former chancellor of the Atlanta University Center and a past president of the University of the District of Columbia

Luther H. Foster, president emeritus of Tuskegee University in Alabama

Eamon Kelly, president of Tulane University in New Orleans

Shirley M. McBay, dean for student affairs at the Massachusetts Institute of Technology

Julius S. Scott Jr., associate general secretary of the United Methodist Church Board of Education and Ministry and former president of Paine College in Augusta, Georgia.

Crawford and his committee spent the next two months reviewing the recommendations made in "Charting a Bold New Future" and meeting with faculty, staff, students and alumni of both Clark College and Atlanta University. The release of the Consolidation Advisory Committee's final report, dated June 16, 1988, was timed so that it went to the full boards of both schools just before the final vote on consolidation. This report would serve as a basis for much of what was discussed and implemented during the transition year, July 1, 1988 to July 1, 1989.

References

Minutes of Clark College Board of Trustees Special Committee on Clark Atlanta University Exploration, November 20, 1987.

Minutes of Joint Board Committee, January 20, 1988.

Interview with Trustee Elridge McMillan, December 3, 2004.

Interview with Patrice Perkins-Hooker and Michael Baskin, April 16, 2004.

Interview with Trustee Myrtle Davis, January 22, 2004.

Interview with Trustee Carl Ware, December 11, 2003.

Minutes of Joint Advisory Committee, May 17, 1988.

CHAPTER 6

Cooperative Spirit Recaptured

From the time I assumed my new duties as president of Clark College on March 1, 1988, the AUC campuses were abuzz with rumors about the discussions between Atlanta University and Clark College. The presidents of the other AUC schools were concerned that they had not been consulted and involved in the deliberations. The idea of Clark College and Atlanta University consolidating had included periods of both formal and informal cooperation as well as times of determined independence.

At the time Clark College and Atlanta University began exploring consolidation, six of the seven presidents were relatively new to the Atlanta University Center and were therefore less familiar with some of the historical institutional and intertwined relationships. They had no connection to a previous era of cooperation when the Cooperative General Science Program, created by Om Puri and endorsed by the AUC Council of Presidents, was offered by Clark College and Fine Arts offered under the leadership of Baldwin Burroughs at Spelman College was offered to all AUC students. It was a time when the only full major in physics was offered by Clark College for all AUC students, when the senior course in chemistry was offered only by Morehouse College and chemists from all schools were informally consulted about the hiring of chemistry faculty at any one of the institutions in an effort to balance specialties and skills across the entire AUC.

These presidents had not been around when students freely took courses on another campus for full academic credit applied at their home institutions or when on any given Friday, at about 4 p.m., the phones started to ring around campus, and the familiar questions were asked: "Are you going to Paschal's?" "What time is everybody heading over to Paschal's?"

In the late sixties and early seventies, a core group of faculty from Atlanta University Center would cram into a few booths at the historic bar and restaurant on Hunter Street (later named Martin Luther King, Jr. Drive) to socialize and unwind. Younger faculty had initiated the ritual, because they had not yet reached the age in which banquets and official engagements took over their Friday nights. As the group grew, age, institutional affiliation or academic discipline did not matter. Friendships and collaboration emerged among scientists, English professors and members of the administrative staff. Some of the best and brightest minds of the day came together in these gatherings. The "dean" of the group was Gerry H. Taylor, Registrar of Atlanta University.

A feeling of community emerged in those days, considered by many to be the heyday of cooperation among the Atlanta University Center schools. Not only did the group socialize together, but the faculty members taught each other's students and benefited from the collective resources that were greater than what a single school could provide on its own. A grassroots, organic cooperation was at work, a sincere collaboration that was never achieved among the six Atlanta University Center schools on an official level.

In 1966, on the recommendations of Kimuel Huggins, chair of Atlanta University's Department of Chemistry, I was contacted by Thomas Jarrett, then Dean of the School of Arts and Sciences at Atlanta University. I was offered the position of assistant professor of chemistry at a nine-month salary of $9,000. To be sure, it was not the money that made me decide to accept the appointment. It had more to do with the fact that McBay and Huggins were there, working in the same building to establish a strong graduate and undergraduate program in chemistry, and the reputation of the AU Center. At that time, there were six graduate students and two full-time members of the Atlanta University chemistry faculty, Huggins and Skevos Tsoukalas, and I thought I could make a real difference.

I was also impressed with the close camaraderie and *esprit de corps* among the faculty in the science and chemistry departments, in particular, but across the board of academic disciplines in the Atlanta University Center. During my initial visit to Atlanta to interview for the position at the University, not only did I meet with Huggins and McBay, who I had known all my life, but also with Charles Merideth and Joe Gayles, two young physical chemists about my age who were already members of the Morehouse College faculty. I also came to know and worked with Lafayette Frederick, chair of the department of biology at Atlanta University, Alfred Spriggs, chair of the department of chemistry, and Om Puri, chair of the department of physics at Clark College; Gloria Anderson, chair of the chemistry department at Morris Brown; and Frederick Mapp, Thomas

Norris and Ronald Sheehy, members of the biology department at Morehouse.

The climate of cooperation among the Atlanta University Center schools seemed to be a natural outflow of the active progressive early 1960s, which saw Atlanta University Center students at the forefront of the civil rights movement.

Competition among the AUC institutions was always below the surface, but it often took a back seat when opportunities arose for the institutions to work together for their common good. Such was the case when science faculties from the AUC institutions collaborated to submit a proposal for a major multi-year grant from the National Institutes of Health called the Biomedical Sciences Research Improvement Program (BISRIP). The Project Director was Joe Johnson, a member of the Atlanta University Chemistry Department. Key members of the team were Lafayette Frederick, Chair of the AU Department of Biology and Winfred Harris, Chair of the Clark College Department of Biology. After numerous meetings from faculty across the Center, a successful proposal was submitted and the AUC was awarded a $5 million grant for five years, a far larger award than the institutions could have garnered separately.

The research faculty from across the Center came together, usually on Saturdays, to discuss BISRIP and other collaborative opportunities, including the creation of the Atlanta University Center Science Research Institute (AUCSRI). The purpose of AUCSRI was to acquire and make available scientific infrastructure support that no one institution could do on its own. This internal cooperation served as a base for the awarding a few years later of a major National

Science Foundation grant to Atlanta University aimed at improving the number of minorities pursuing careers in the physical sciences, mathematics and engineering in the AUC and at twenty neighboring undergraduate institutions in the Southeast called the Resource Center for Science and Engineering. One of the components of that program included the Saturday Science Academy which was pioneered in Atlanta in 1977 under the direction of Melvin Webb for elementary school students, grades 3-8.

The compatibility of personalities made the interaction across institutions work, and led to the formation of an AUC Faculty Club, which operated for several years at a house on Beckwith Street for AUC faculty to convene for lunch and social gatherings. As years passed and faculty and leaders came and went, the collaborative atmosphere began to erode.

The climate that emerged was not one that would welcome a consolidation or increased collaboration between any two of the institutions without the prior review and approval of the AUC Council of presidents. All but two of the members of the Council balked initially at the mere idea of Clark College and Atlanta University coming together. At the time the council consisted of Charles Merideth, AUC chancellor; Dorcas Bowles, Interim President, Atlanta University; Johnnetta Cole, President, Spelman; James Costen, President, The Interdenominational Theological Center; Leroy Keith, President, Morehouse; Louis Sullivan, President, Morehouse School of Medicine; Calvert Smith, President, Morris Brown; and me, as Clark's new president. The presidents were surprised by the rapid pace of negotiations and concerned over the number of questions about everything from use of building space to

AUC membership fees. There was also concern that the consolidation of two schools would lead to a renewed call for the others to follow suit.

Although the idea of bringing the Atlanta University Center schools together as one institution had been around nearly as long as the schools themselves, it had always been brought up more frequently off campus than on. "I know the Atlanta business community very much wanted to see consolidation there on account of fund-raising," said Cecil Alexander, a prominent Atlanta architect and businessman who had served on the boards of Atlanta University and Clark College. "It would just simplify things. There was a general feeling that (the combined Center schools) would be stronger."

The desire for a single university structure among Atlanta's black institutions went beyond Atlanta's business community, and reached as far back as the 1920s. At that time, national education leaders began to lobby Atlanta University, Morehouse and Spelman to come together to eliminate competition and duplication of services. Described as a "proposed merger" in Clarence A. Bacote's *The Story of Atlanta University*, the effort instead resulted in the Affiliation Agreement of 1929. Originally involving only Atlanta University, Morehouse and Spelman, in later years Clark University (which became Clark College), Morris Brown College and the Interdenominational Theological Center were invited into the affiliation.

Under the 1929 agreement, Atlanta University phased out its undergraduate program and became the graduate school for the all-male Morehouse College and the all-female Spelman College. The agreement also provided for the establishment of interlocking boards of trustees, a shared library and administrative building and a united summer school program coordinated by Atlanta University.

For a short period of time, John Hope served as president of Morehouse College and Atlanta University. Through the years, buildings were shared, and at one point, the presidents' offices for Morehouse, Spelman and Atlanta University were all located in Harkness Hall. Still today the building, which now houses the administration offices for Clark Atlanta University, contains vaults labeled "Morehouse," "Spelman" and "Atlanta University" on its first floor.

In 1956, the 1929 agreement was revised to create the Atlanta University Center Consortium with the appointment of an Executive Director whose responsibility was to oversee center-wide programs and serve as convener of the Council of Presidents to discuss joint programs.

The level of cooperation varied over the early half of the twentieth century, becoming strongest during the 1960s. Attention from the outside also peaked during this time with another lobbying effort to try to get the AUC schools joined as one institution. Some of the same young professors who in the mid-sixties planted the seeds for grassroots cooperation among AUC schools would also find themselves involved in the most aggressive attempt to combine the institutions up to that time.

In the late sixties, the Council of Presidents initiated a two-year study intended to review how the AUC schools should work better together. Funded by the Ford Foundation, the study was completed in 1970. Referred to now as the Eurich Report, named after the study's steering committee chairman, Alvin C. Eurich, it was conducted by a panel of education experts led by Julius Scott and assembled by the Academy for Educational Development, a nonprofit organization that focuses on solving social issues. The final report recommended radical changes aimed at creating one HBCU in Atlanta.

While initially supporting a study on how the six AUC schools could work together and combine resources, the Council of Presidents backed away from many of the report's ideas for the simple reason that, from their point of view, the ideas went too far. The majority of the recommendations depended on the existing presidents and boards of trustees relinquishing much of their power and independence in deference to a newly created board that would oversee the Center. The focus was on creating one voice for the Center schools, and eventually one school.

The final version of the Eurich Report concluded that no single institution in the Atlanta University Center had the resources "now, nor can it expect to gather them in the future, to develop as a unique educational center for Black Americans independently of all other Center institutions. We believe that this potential is inherent, however, in the six institutions jointly."

As part of its assessment, the panel held numerous focus groups with faculty, staff, students and community members and identified 13 problems that had to be dealt with effectively. Among them, the Center needed to eliminate duplication of curriculum and services, make better use of the physical facilities and their surrounding land, change the collective mind-set to allow for successful cooperative efforts and speak with one voice when dealing with city, county and federal agencies.

The panel created a university structure and list of required changes that the Council of Presidents chose not to follow. As sponsors of the Eurich Report, the Ford Foundation backed the panel's findings that the schools should come together and put forth a $20 million grant to support the implementation of the Eurich Report recommendations.

The Eurich panel and Council of Presidents were gathered for a three-day retreat in Nassau, Bahamas, to discuss the recommendations and a series of proposals for restructuring the Atlanta University Center. While there was overall interest in improving cooperation among the schools, the Council of Presidents was also motivated by the $20 million to find a way to increase collaboration. The council stopped short of many of the Eurich report recommendations, and instead created the Atlanta University Center, Inc., complete with its own board of trustees. The AUC would be supported through fees from the six member schools and would be led by a separate chancellor. The Center would oversee shared resources such as the administrative data processing center, the bookstore and the office of public safety. The AUC, which would grow to seven schools in 1982 with the creation of Morehouse School of Medicine, would also later control a new central library, built in 1980-81 with a major personal gift from Coca-Cola magnate Robert W. Woodruff.

When the presidents of ITC, Morehouse, Morehouse School of Medicine, Morris Brown and Spelman learned of the pending consolidation of Atlanta University and Clark College, they may have experienced what amounted to a flashback to the idea of full consolidation.

The presidents of Morehouse and Spelman were especially concerned with existing agreements on joint use of facilities, particularly Harkness Hall and Trevor Arnett Hall, the site of the old AUC library. Morris Brown's president was concerned about whether the reversionary clause between Morris Brown and Atlanta University would be activated by the consolidation. That portion of the land occupied by Morris Brown had originally been owned and occupied by Atlanta University, and the reversionary clause in the deed provided for the land to revert to Atlanta University should Morris Brown ever cease to exist as an educational institution.

The president of the Morehouse School of Medicine was concerned about the 1929 agreement that authorized graduate programs to be offered exclusively by Atlanta University, as well as the impact the consolidation would have on a proposed joint M.D.-Ph.D. program that would be shared by the two schools. The AUC chancellor was interested in the financial obligation the new school would have in terms of fees paid to the AUC. Would they be equivalent to the fees Clark College and Atlanta University had been paying separately? The library endowment, managed by Atlanta University, was also an AUC concern. All the institutions requested a delay in the consolidation to provide more time for review of the impact of the decision on their respective institutions. All their concerns were taken *seriously.* All the AUC presidents had their own obligations to a board of trustees, a faculty and administrative staff, students and alumni. The need to represent separate constituencies often put the presidents at odds on specific issues.

All the issues raised by the Council of Presidents were thoroughly researched by the legal staff and resolved. An extensive review of archived legal documents took place, and each AUC institution was advised in writing that there was no breach of the Affiliation Agreements *of 1929 and 1956.* These agreements in no way prohibited member institutions from consolidating.

- Contractual obligations of Atlanta University and Clark College, by operation of law, would become the obligation of Clark Atlanta University.
- The financial assessment of Clark Atlanta University as a member institution of the AUC would be determined based on a new formula that recognized it as an undergraduate and graduate institution.
- The Clark Atlanta University board would transfer the $600,000 library endowment to the AUC, Inc., to support operation of the Robert W. Woodruff Library.

A review of archived documents revealed unequivocally that Harkness Hall was owned by Atlanta University, with space allowed for the beneficial use of Atlanta University, Spelman College and Morehouse College. With the construction of the Robert W. Woodruff Library in 1981, Atlanta University had no further obligation to share space in Trevor Arnett. The matter of space was then reduced to individual agreements, which were worked out between Clark Atlanta University and Morehouse and Spelman colleges, independently.

The major concerns of the member institutions were addressed institution by institution, and each by vote of its board approved the admission of CAU as a consolidated entity to the AUC during the

1988-89 academic year. Because pending issues with the Commission on Colleges of the Southern Association of Colleges and Schools required more time to address, the effective date of the consolidation was shifted to July 1989.

Atlanta University and Clark College held separate Commencement Exercises in 1988. However, in May 1989, prior to the formal consolidation and as part of a deliberate and progressive process, Clark Atlanta University held its first Commencement Exercise at the Fox Theater with one speaker. Degrees were awarded by each institution. On the recommendation by Charles Stephens, then Vice President for Development, to the Administrative Council, Baccalaureate Services were resumed the following year. The speaker for the first Commencement was General Colin Powell. Honorary degrees were awarded to Powell, Anne Cox Chambers, Lou Rawls (degrees from both AU and CC), Reatha Clark King and Carl Ware. Over the ensuing 15 years, the University awarded over 12,000 undergraduate and graduate degrees and 36 honorary degrees (see appendix for list). Members of the 1989 graduating class were offered the opportunity to receive the name of the parent institution under which they enrolled or the new institution on their diploma. The overwhelming majority of the graduates chose the new institution, Clark Atlanta University.

References

Interview with Trustee Cecil Alexander, January 15, 2004.

Bacote, Clarence A. *The Story of Atlanta University: A Century of Service,* 1865-1965. Princeton University Press, 1969.

Interview with Julius Scott, Study Director of Eurich Report.

CHAPTER 7

The Transition Year

My home telephone rang at 6:30 on a November morning in 1988. A voice on the other end was asking, "When are you coming to Cairo?" Cairo? The question came as a shot out of the blue, and I really did not know what to say. I had not yet been inaugurated as president of the university, but I was already intensely involved in operational and accreditation issues. Now, here was a man I didn't know talking to me about a $25-million contract I had no knowledge of and telling me to make a trip to Cairo, Egypt within the next two weeks.

I had already been briefed on the status of most of the federal projects, including the matching requirement of a $5-million grant from the Department of Education to renovate Ware-Bumstead Halls. However, during the Luther Williams presidency, Atlanta University had also applied for and received a $25-million five-year contract from United States Agency for International Development (USAID) to provide technical assistance to the Ministry of Health of Egypt for a Child Survival Project.

News of this project confirmed my sense that the transition year of consolidation required carefully managing the internal challenges without ignoring the two schools' relationships to the outside world. The threat loomed daily that important projects, people and programs might slip through the cracks. While hundreds of people were wrapped up in the daily on-campus challenges of combining two major institutions, we had critical external relationships that needed nurturing, too.

To help guide the daunting consolidation process, we created an eighteen-member Steering Committee chaired by Vernon Crawford that included equal representation from the two legacy institutions which engaged some of the most highly respected members of the faculty and staff, along with two students and two alumni. We also sought input through weekly roundtable discussions that became known as the Holly Hill Dialogues. Holly Hill (named by Belle Dennard, the former First Lady of AU) was the residence of the Atlanta University president, but during the transition year I was residing in the Clark College president's home.

The well-attended talks were held from 7-9 p.m., and along with other members of the steering committee, I attended most of them. Faculty, staff and students were invited in small groups to discuss whatever concerns they had about the consolidation. "Whether they were pleased with the answers or not, they had the opportunity to express themselves," said Pearlie Dove, who coordinated the Holly Hill Dialogues and took copious notes.

The consolidation hurdles we faced ranged from synchronizing the calendars of two separate institutions to preserving the accreditation of the consolidated entity and writing governance documents for the new institution. We had the odd problem of having duplicate resources in certain areas. We were faced with two of everything from department chairs and deans to administrative officers and staff. Two separate computer systems needed to be merged. Offices that accommodated six needed to house ten or twelve, so we were faced with the need to renovate space to handle the consolidated staff.

We tried to make the streamlining process as fair as possible. We sought input from senior staff and faculty from both institutions and made an effort to incorporate gender and institutional balance in all our decisions. For the most part, during the transitional year, Atlanta University continued to operate as a graduate school; and Clark College, as an undergraduate school.

We were also able to implement all the action items agreed to by the Joint Board Committee and completed the legal due diligence process to protect the names and marks in perpetuity for both legacy institutions, Atlanta University and Clark College. The colors at Clark College were red and black; at Atlanta University; crimson and gray. So, red, black and gray were chosen as the colors for the new entity. In 1991, C. Eric Lincoln wrote a song for the new university, "Reign, Clark Atlanta" (the music was written a few years later by Roland Carter) but in the meantime, both school songs would be played and sung at all ceremonial events. The mottos from the two legacy institutions were retained, "Culture for Service" (Clark College) and "I'll find a way or make one" (Atlanta University) and the symbols from both institutions were incorporated into the new seal. The outer circle of the seal bears the name and founding date of the new University. In the field of the seal is an open book representing the search for and transmission of knowledge and more specifically the enlightenment of the Bible. On the left page are inscribed the date of the founding of Atlanta University and its traditional emblems of the sword of truth and the torch of knowledge. On the right page are the founding date of Clark College and its emblem of a lamp. Both the torch and the lamp signify knowledge and the illumination of the mind.

A new logo was created and the Clark College Panther was adopted as mascot. Atlanta University did not have an athletic program and did not have a mascot.

The Clark Atlanta University board first met to transact business of the new entity in October 1988. The keynote speakers for the two-day retreat were Samuel D. Procter, Julius S. Scott and Vernon Crawford. At that meeting, the founding board for the new university consisted of the following persons:

Chairman: Carl Ware
Vice Chairman, Thomas Cordy
Secretary: Myrtle Davis
President: Thomas W. Cole, Jr.
Trustees:

Charles S. Ackerman	Deloris P. Alridge	Cecil Alexander
Marvin S. Arrington	William H. Boone	Tyra Boyd
Lawrence Cowart	A. W. Dahlberg III	Harold E. Doley, Jr.
Lamond Godwin	Mel H. Gregory	T. Marshall Hahn
Paul L. Hackett	Cornelius L. Henderson	Michael R. Hollis
Hylan T. Hubbard III	Morris F. X. Jeff, Jr.	Major J. Jones
James R. Kuse	Carson Lee	Elridge McMillan
The Hon. Sam Nunn	James D. Palmer	Jamyee C. Pleasant
George R. Puskar	Margaret L. Roach	Leonard H. Roberts
C. E. Steel	Sydney Topol	Welcome Watson
Prentiss Q. Yancy		

One management team called the Administrative Council was formed to lead the consolidated university, which included equal numbers of senior administrative staff from both institutions. Dorcas Bowles, Kofi Bota, Nathaniel Pollard and Getchel Caldwell represented Atlanta University, and Winfred Harris, Larry Earvin, Gloria James, Om Puri, Roy Bolton and Charles Stephens came from Clark College. Conrad Snowden, first provost of the university, and Carl Spight, special assistant to the president, were new to the administrative team and started their work in late spring of 1988. In subsequent years, the academic deans, director of human resources and general counsel were added as members of the Administrative Council. Both institutions brought multitalented administrative experiences during the early years, including Larry Earvin who served for a time as Vice President for Student Affairs, Associate Provost and then Dean of the School of Arts and Sciences, William Boone served as Dean of the Graduate School and Alexa Henderson was Dean for Undergraduate Studies and who served for a year as Interim Dean of the School of Arts and sciences following Earvin's departure. Doris Weathers joined the administrative team as Vice President for Student Affairs. She ended her career at the University many years later as Vice President for Institutional Effectiveness and an expert on SACS accreditation standards. The spiritual leader during this period was Rev. Paul Easley, University Chaplain.

While the Administrative Council was leading the day-to-day operations of the new consolidated university, the Consolidation Steering Committee worked on the broader issues that were associated with consolidation and development of the final structure for the University. The Committee was critical to the success of the transition. Composed of an equal number of members from both legacy institutions, the committee was chaired by Vernon Crawford. The co-chair was Pearlie Dove. Additionally, annual retreats for members of the Administrative Council were held, usually off site, to review annual plans program by program and school by school. Some were facilitated, but most were not.

Crawford and I had a long professional history, dating back to the mid-1970s when he was chair of the Department of Physics at Georgia Tech and I was chair of the Department of Chemistry at Atlanta University. When I was appointed provost and vice president for academic affairs in 1977, I called him to ask for his advice. He had been serving in that position at Georgia Tech for several years. He took me to lunch, gave me some good advice and we met periodically after that until I went to West Virginia. Crawford was then appointed Chancellor of the Georgia Board of Regents. He was one of the first persons who called to congratulate me following the announcement of my appointment as president of Clark College. Though he had retired by that time, he said he had heard the rumor about bringing Clark College and Atlanta University together and asked me if there was anything he might do to help. I took him up on his offer.

Pearlie Dove was longtime chair of the Department of Education at Clark College and had coordinated at least two self-studies for reaffirmation of accreditation by the Southern Association of Colleges and Schools. Among other accomplishments, she was considered an expert in accreditation, and she provided leadership to a department of education with a strong reputation for producing students who passed the state teachers' education exam on the first attempt.

Crawford and Dove worked very well together. Their work with the steering committee resulted in a series of documents and recommendations that positioned the university for the phase of its operation as a single institution that would begin on July 1, 1989. They examined every issue; no stone was left unturned. The agenda of the Steering Committee was strategically designed to coincide with the SACS reaffirmation criteria, and the subcommittees were created so that following the transition year, the University would have the basic documentation needed for accreditation as a new institution.

The pursuit of accreditation turned out to be more complicated than we anticipated initially. During the 1987-88 academic year, Clark College was well along with its 10-year accreditation review process. For Atlanta University, permission was granted from the Commission on Colleges to delay the process for one year because of uncertainty in leadership at Atlanta University at that time. Given that Clark College had already gone through the process and Atlanta University was continued in accredited status for another year, we requested from SACS that further self-study activities be delayed until the consolidation had been consummated. At that time, the accreditation guidelines for institutions considering consolidation or merger were not well-defined by the Commission. The Commission developed a new set of criteria to cover such cases, called "substantive change," to apply when an institution altered its academic offerings. In our case, the substantive change involved consolidating a graduate school with an undergraduate school.

In June 1988, we were advised by the Commission on Colleges to defer any formal actions that would result in consolidation of the two institutions until each had successfully completed its application for reaffirmation and its accreditation status could be affirmed by the Commission on Colleges at the annual meeting in December 1988. That decision was disappointing to us. It meant the institution had to follow through with the Clark College self-study review and an equivalent process for Atlanta University as a separate activity. In addition to serving as president of Clark College, I was named President of Atlanta University in July 1988 to expedite this process. I became President of Clark Atlanta University in October 1988, however, the effective date of the consolidation was July 1, 1989.

In the fall of 1988, Atlanta University had resumed its preparation of the self-study report, under the leadership of William Denton, anticipating a visit from the commission prior to the December annual meeting. A visiting committee came to the university to review the status of preparation and readiness for substantive change according to the new SACS guidelines.

On December 11, 1988, university personnel met with the Commission on Colleges to present the case for consolidation in response to recommendations and questions resulting from a visiting committee that met at the University on December 1, 1988. The University was represented at that meeting by Carl Ware and Thomas Cordy, co-chairs of the board; Dorcas Bowles, former acting president of Atlanta University and then vice president for student affairs; Vernon Crawford, chair of the Consolidation Steering Committee; Winfred Harris, executive vice president; and President Cole.

All the SACS commissioners were present in the room. Most of them had no idea how monumental was this decision to consolidate the two institutions. It was a somewhat intimidating environment for me, because so much was at stake. I presented the case for consolidation to create Clark Atlanta University, with strong supporting comments from Ware, Cordy and the administrative staff who were present. The presentation outlined every step in the process that had been completed to date, as well as what was yet to be done. We outlined a timetable, responded to questions and recommendations from the visiting committee and the commission and detailed our financial management plan. We presented an analysis of our facilities, a preliminary draft of the administrative organizational structure of the new institution and a draft of a three-year capital development plan.

Crawford, who was well known to most of the members of the commission, made follow-up comments to the presentation. His involvement was especially helpful in addressing the skepticism of some members of the commission who were unfamiliar with the history of the Atlanta University Center and why the consolidation of the two institutions made sense. Having the co-chairs of the board present to make comments was critical, as was having in place a president for the consolidated university. There were two options available for the Commission to consider. Either accept Clark Atlanta University as an accredited institution because of the individual accreditations of Clark College and Atlanta University or accept the new entity as a candidate for accreditation as a new institution. We preferred the first option.

The advantage of the first option would have been accreditation for Clark Atlanta University immediately for the normal ten-year cycle. The second option would limit accreditation to five years. The Commission approved the second option. Admission to candidacy meant the institution was accredited for the awarding of degrees based on the current status of Clark College and Atlanta University, but would have to receive reaffirmation of accreditation in five years.

During the transition year, it was important early on to write and get approved the needed governance documents that would facilitate decision-making at the new university. Under the leadership of Provost Snowden, and with input from the faculty, Deans and Administrative Council, a Faculty Handbook was written and the structure for the University Senate, the highest policy-making authority at the University, and an Administrative Procedures Manual were developed. The Handbook took care to reconcile the difference in tenure requirements from the two parent institutions to minimize conflict and legal issues when tenure decisions had to be made. Fortunately, with the input of the Faculty Assembly, the faculty governance entity, the Staff Assembly and the University Senate, few issues were created that caused a major problem that had not already been passed through legal review. The Provost and I met monthly with the Faculty Assembly, and separately with the Staff assembly leadership, which elected its own chairs, and seven times a year with the University Senate, which I chaired.

Another critical development during the year was the combination of the two alumni associations. A Plan was developed and approved by each individual association to dissolve the separate associations and combine, effective July 1, 1990. This plan reflected the extraordinary leadership, commitment and comradeship of the two presidents of the respective alumni associations, Maurice Fitts Page (Clark College) and Robert Davis (Atlanta University). The alumni also recommended the discontinuance of the practice of observing a separate Charter Day in October for Atlanta University and a Founder's Day in March for Clark College, but to combine them into one celebration for Clark Atlanta Univer University on the third week in April.

The faculty and staff leadership were absolutely critical during this early formative years of the consolidation. The first five chairs of the Faculty Assembly were Gloria Blackwell, Carolyn Fowler, Ora Cooks, Gloria Mixon, and David Dorsey. For the Staff Assembly, the first five presidents were Sandra Flowers, Gwendolyn Callaway, Alimah Maloud, Susan Gibson and LaVorius Mullens.

The 1989-90 Student Government leaders, Beverly Richardson (Graduate) and Mark Tyler (Undergraduate) joined forces with the vision of creating a single organization to serve the entire student body. As one indication of that unity, they spoke from a combined speech at my inauguration.

The pressures of the transition year were not all connected to consolidation issues. What became known as the Egyptian Child Survival Project (ESP) would stretch us in other ways. When I received that early morning phone call from Dr. Ragheb Dewidar, Egyptian Minister of Health, I learned that if we did not travel to Egypt by the end of that month, Clark Atlanta University might forfeit its role in the project as prime contractor.

The main objective of the project was improving the health of the Egyptian people through reduction of the morbidity and mortality rates of infants and children under five years of age and women of child-bearing age. The proposal came from the AU

School of Business, but the lead faculty member who wrote the grant application was Samy Sidky, a native Egyptian whose position had been eliminated during the period of financial exigency that was declared by Atlanta University in 1987.

Later that year, Atlanta University sought technical advice on the project from the Carter Center. The Center sent a team to Cairo to evaluate the project and determine what role, if any, it might play in assisting the university with the contract.

Once the details of the grant and the breadth of Clark Atlanta's role were explained, I contacted Sidky, who was still living in Atlanta and still interested in the project. We scheduled a trip to Cairo. I also contacted Dr. James Sarn, a medical doctor on the USAID-Cairo staff who specialized in international development work. For more help on the project, I turned to Kofi Bota and Frank Cummings, a professor in the Department of Chemistry who was just returning from a sabbatical leave. A week later, Cummings, Sidky and I went to Cairo to sign documents that detailed the work that would be done. The trip launched one of the most successful and rewarding professional ventures I have ever experienced.

None of us had much experience in international development work. I selected Cummings because I knew him to be a person of integrity who loved working with details. Having served as a project director of a major federal grant myself, I knew about the detailed administrative requirements involved in directing a project of this magnitude. We would need someone who had experience in managing grants and the ability to handle the complex details and paperwork that would be associated with a USAID contract. I wanted someone I could trust with such a large contract. Sidky further briefed us on the details of the project during our flight to Cairo.

In Cairo we met with the Minister of Health and his staff and then with the staff of the Child Survival Project, gifted Egyptian professionals deeply committed to the cause of Egyptian child survival. We met with Jim Sarn, who turned out to be an outstanding colleague. He, too, was committed to the project and wanted to see the activities implemented for the right reason: for the children of Egypt. He was very experienced with international development work on health and gave us excellent advice and support. I signed the contract and we returned to Atlanta immediately.

As soon as we recovered from our three-day turnaround trip, we met with colleagues at the Carter Center to share our concerns about the project and its challenges. Carter Center advisers cautioned that the project could not be implemented as designed in the initial proposal by Atlanta University. We then made changes in staffing requirements, and after receiving approval from USAID, Cummings was appointed as project manager for the home office with responsibilities for overall coordination of the project.

Several early mistakes were made in the Child Survival Project, but the University recovered, thanks in large part to the hard work of Cummings and Sarn and to the great fortune of a casual conversation with Haskell Ward, a Clark College alumnus who was experienced in African development work. As it turned out, Haskell had prior relationships with the U. S. Ambassador to Egypt and many of the USAID staff. After a preliminary visit to Cairo, he agreed to serve as a consultant and my emissary to Egypt for this project for several years. Cummings traveled often to Egypt, and Ward visited the project biannually to ascertain progress and to resolve problems before they escalated, as was the case during the early years. I visited Cairo annually to meet with the U.S. Ambassador, the Minister of Health and the project staff to assure that the University was still performing the objectives of the project and satisfying our role in providing the best technical assistance available from around the world. After the fourth year, we identified an excellent Chief of Party, Reginald Gipson, an M.D./Ph.D. who, provided excellent leadership for 3 years and tremendously reduced the level of anxiety and challenges of the day-to-day operation in Cairo. The University's credibility, reputation and project mission were at stake, and we went to great lengths to make this project a success. The project eventually was awarded an additional $16 million in contracts, and work was extended for five more years.

The final assessment of the Egypt CSP by the USAID in 1995 concluded that CSP contributed to reduced infant, child and maternal mortality in Egypt. The 1995 Demographic and Health Survey (DHS) showed an average of 35 percent decline in infant mortality and 59 percent decline in child mortality over a 10-year period covered by the contract, leaving behind a very significant improvement in the health status of children and a foundation for improved maternal health.

The reputation that Clark Atlanta gained in Egypt and in the international health and development community with such organizations as USAID, the World Health Organization (WHO) made it worth the time and investment and helped reaffirm the importance of the Gray Amendment (named after William H. Gray when he was a member of Congress and introduced the legislation) in the awarding of USAID contracts to Historically Black Colleges and Universities. It also complemented the University's effort to pursue numerous international programs in Africa and throughout the world and helped support the creation of the School of International Affairs and the Office of Institutionalization and help sustain the Office of International Programs. It helped propel Clark Atlanta University to international recognition with several individual and institutional contracts that were periodically identified with numerous parts of the world because of the long standing involvement and commitment of faculty to Africa, Caribbean and the African Diaspora; among them were Richard Long, Herschelle Challenor, Shelby Lewis, Kofi Bota, Earle Clowney, Earl Picard, Mack Jones, David Dorsey, and Robert Holmes, in efforts prior to the consolidation.

References

FINAL Assessment of the Egyptian Child Survival Project (263-0203), August, 1996, U. S. Agency for International Development (Project No. 936-3024)

Reception at president's home: L - R: Ingrid Saunders Jones, Lamond Godwin, Mary Ware, Marilyn Keough, Donald Keough, Carl Ware, Brenda Cole, Thomas Cole, Bryant Gumbel and George Puskar

CHAPTER 8

The New University

The transition year (1989-90) for the new university was a year full of excitement, starting in September with a wonderfully planned and executed inauguration, co-chaired by Alexa Henderson and Getchel Caldwell. Highlights of the inaugural week included community activities and events designed to help connect the University to the larger Atlanta community. Speakers included Eric Bloch, Director of the National Science Foundation, Mae Jemison, the first (and only) African American female astronaut, Shirley Malcolm, American Association for the Advancement of Science, Philip Uri Treisman, Director of the Dana Center at The University of California-Berkeley and Emanuel Lewis, then a student at the University. During the festivities, other highlights included contributions in the arts and humanities, writings of the African Diaspora, music from Armenta Adams and the Pan People and a student production in Underground Atlanta led by Emmanuel Lewis, then a CAU student. The newly commissioned Anthem, "This Day," written by Marvin Curtis was introduced. (It was sung by the University Community Choir under the leadership of Thomas Hager and by the CAU Philharmonic Society under the direction of Glynn Halsey at every Founders Day Convocation through March 2002.

There were other defining moments during the year, including the first visit by Nelson Mandela and a number of key academic appointments. New academic deans were named: Charles Churchwell, School of Library and Information Studies (Churchwell also served a term as Interim Provost and served simultaneously for a short period as Dean and Director of the Woodruff Library); William Scott, School of Arts and Sciences; Edward Irons, School of Business Administration; Lou Beasley, School of Social Work; and Melvin Webb, School of Education. Webb had served previously as Dean at Clark College and Director of the Saturday Science Academy and Pre-college component of the Atlanta Resource Center.

The first Chief Financial Officer was Thomas Poitier who came to the University from PMG Accounting and Auditing Firm in Atlanta. He was followed by Donald Murphy, CEO of The Wesley Peachtree Group, a local accounting and auditing firm. Murphy was intimately familiar with the books and accounting system at Atlanta University just prior to consolidation and was key to implementing a single accounting system that integrated the endowments and financial records from both institutions. Additional members of the administration included Debra McCurdy, Assistant Provost, and Sherman Jones, who followed Churchwell as Provost, Kofi Bota (Interim), Yvonne Freeman and Winfred Harris.

Under the leadership of Gloria James, Self-Study Director, the University received notification from the Southern Association of Colleges and Schools (SACS) in December that Clark Atlanta University had met all requirements for accreditation as a combined institution, effective January 1, 1990. In addition to the general SACS accreditation, the University had successful accreditation visits for all four professional schools and hosted six external accreditation site visits, which provided the initial accreditation for the undergraduate programs in Allied Health and Business Administration, and the Master's Program in Public Administration. Programs at the Master's degree level, in Business Administration, Social Work Library Science and Education all received reaccreditation that year.

Enrollment in the fall of 1990 reached 3,507, an increase of ten percent over 1987. Graduate enrollment was 968. Overall, applications were up by 107 percent and the average SAT score had increased 100 points. The student body, two-thirds of whom were female, came from every state and thirty-six foreign countries. Eighty-five percent were full-time students, fifty percent came from Georgia, and six percent were international students.

Following the approval by the Board of Trustees, the University began using its new governance documents. The University ended the year with a balanced operating budget with total revenues of $50.7 million, compared to $40 million in the previous year. Since the consolidation, the endowment had increased from $15.9 million to $18.2 million.

During that year, the faculty published six books and participated in more than $20 million in external federal funding. The University initiated the Partners in a Planned Community, a collaboration with John Hope/University Homes, a public housing complex located adjacent to the campus. Under the leadership of Dean Lou Beasley of the School of Social Work, the project was funded with a planning grant from the Ford Foundation and support from the Aetna Company with a gift that was facilitated by Trustee Marvin Arrington. The University Community Development Corporation

(UCDC) was created as a catalyst and coordinating entity for community-based efforts aimed at redevelopment of the AUC community and received a major start-up grant of $215,000 from the Ford Foundation. The University also completed a facilities master plan and began operating the largest Head Start Program in the Southeast. Two years later, William Allison and Ben Brown, the staff of the UCDC, led our negotiations with Mr. James Paschal to purchase the Paschal Restaurant and Hotel in 1994 for graduate student housing just prior to the Olympics. Alumni contributions that year neared $400,000 for the first time.

With the support of a federal loan, Ware and Bumstead Halls were renovated and a new 225-bed graduate dormitory was constructed on Beckwith Street. The University was the proud recipient of a marvelous gift of writings and photographs from Pauline Young, which included memorabilia from her aunt and uncle, Alice Dunbar Nelson and Paul Laurence Dunbar.

Also during 1990, the University received a grant of $400,000 from the Georgia-Pacific Company to help jump-start the revitalization of the Vine City area. This grant was used for renovation of ten of the eighteen faculty homes on Beckwith Street (known as Faculty Row) that had been vacant for years. Georgia-Pacific, H. R Russell Construction Company and First National Bank of Atlanta partnered in this effort. This was the first activity of the university's initiatives to start the restoration of the surrounding community. Within one year, all the homes were given a facelift, and occupied by faculty and staff of the university. The chimes in the bell tower on Harkness Hall were repaired and started ringing on the hour and all buildings on the old AU quadrangle received a much needed facelift.

Another special event during the year was the Thirtieth Anniversary Celebration of the Student Movement of the Atlanta University Center. On March 9, 1960, "The Appeal for Human Rights," prepared by Atlanta University Center students, penned by Rosalyn Pope, SGA President at Spelman College, and signed by the student government officers from all the AUC Schools, was printed as a full-page ad in *The Atlanta Journal-Constitution* and other publications. It is heralded as the official beginning of the Atlanta Student Movement, which brought a year of peaceful protests against segregated public accommodations in Atlanta, the South and the country.

"The Appeal for Human Rights" marks an extraordinary and unprecedented example of collaboration and commitment among the students in the Atlanta University Center. The document begins:

"We do not intend to wait placidly for those rights, which are already legally and morally ours, to be meted out to us one at a time. Today's youth will not sit by submissively, while being denied all of the rights, privileges and joys of life. We want to state clearly and unequivocally that we cannot tolerate, in professing democracy and among people professing Christianity, the discriminatory conditions, which the Negro is living today in Atlanta, Georgia—supposedly one of the most progressive cities in the South."

The lunch counter sit-ins and peaceful protest marches united the students on the campuses of Atlanta University, the

Interdenominational Theological Center and Clark, Morehouse, Morris Brown and Spelman colleges. It was only fitting that nearly thirty years later, a weekend celebration honoring these students should be one of the first official events hosted by the new Clark Atlanta University.

The protests were a remarkable accomplishment by students who had never been thanked publicly by the city, by the schools or by anybody. We could not let this thirtieth anniversary pass without a celebration or recognition of the student leaders and community leaders who helped make this movement possible and successful without bloodshed and violence. This was also a personal mission for First Lady, Brenda Cole, who as a 17-year-old student at Spelman College participated in these very student protests.

The Clark Atlanta University committee invited others from the AUC and recognized student leaders and protest participants, bringing many of them together with civic and university center leaders of 1960 and 1990 for a weekend of honoring and remembering.

The two-day event, held March 16-18, 1990, drew people from around the country. Honorees included former student protest leaders Lonnie King, Benjamin Brown, Herschelle Challenor, Otis Moss, Jr. and Julian Bond. The Reverend Jesse Jackson, Journalist Charlayne Hunter-Gault who, along with Hamilton Holmes integrated the University of Georgia, and Ambassador Andrew Young were also program participants.

The reunion weekend included a panel discussion led by student leaders, an awards banquet and a memorial service honoring student and civic leaders who had died. But more than anything, it was a weekend to remember a turbulent time in our history, and reflect on how far we had come and recognize those who had helped make it possible. A memorial was placed in front of Trevor Arnett Hall.

Six weeks prior to the first Atlanta sit-in, the nation watched four black freshmen from North Carolina A&T sit at the whites-only lunch counter at Woolworth's in Greensboro, North Carolina. Store operators responded by closing the counter. It was this quiet, deliberate protest against inequities and segregation that spurred the Atlanta University Center students to action in Atlanta. In February 1960, members of the Committee on the Appeal for Human Rights met with the Council of Presidents and informed them of their plans. Dr. Rufus Clement, then president of Atlanta University, suggested that the students publish their grievances before beginning the sit-ins. On March 15, 1960, nearly 200 black students led by Morehouse student Lonnie King staged sit-ins at nine cafeterias and restaurants, Atlanta City Hall, the state capitol, the Fulton County courthouse and the train station. The event was a peaceful expression by well-dressed, mostly middle-class students. The women wore dresses, and some of the men were in suits. Seventy people were arrested that day, including the Rev. A.D. King, the younger brother of Martin Luther King Jr.

Little did we know when the University opened up the 1990s with a tribute to the Civil Rights sit-ins that Atlanta would soon be the center once again of racial unrest. Like 1960, Atlanta University

Center students would be at the center of the action. Unlike 1960, it would be far from peaceful.

On Friday afternoon, May 1, 1992, at the end of what had turned out to be a long, stressful week, the near-deafening sound of nearly a dozen helicopters could be heard hovering overhead. For students on campus, the sound issued a challenge. This was day three of intense student reaction to a California court's acquittal of four white Los Angeles police officers of all but one charge in the savage beating of a black man, Rodney King. The National Guard had been called to the Atlanta University Center, ordered to keep students under control and block their passage into downtown Atlanta.

I knew the Rodney King decision was going to be problematic for some students, and that there were going to be demonstrations of some sort. But, I did not anticipate how upset and angry the students were going to be when that decision came down. Students felt angry, first at the California verdict, then at Atlanta leaders who forbade them to protest after a march downtown the day before turned violent and destructive. Students from all Atlanta University Center schools gathered on Clark Atlanta University's campus, a central point of the six campuses. It was a volatile situation.

The controversial verdict was handed down on Wednesday, April 29. Shortly before midnight, about 100 students gathered at the state Capitol, staging a protest to express their outrage and pain over the decision. I stayed in my office through most of the night, preparing for a board of trustees meeting on Friday and keeping up with the students' actions through phone calls from people like Getchel Caldwell, who followed the students to the Capitol, my son, Thomas, then a student at CAU, and Greg Sims, president of the CAU student government association. They were with the students, and made periodic phone calls to update me on the situation. It proved to be the first of several long nights as students struggled with the same emotional turmoil that gripped the rest of the country. On Thursday morning, the Council of Presidents scheduled a hastily called meeting inviting the leadership of the student government associations from all the AUC schools to meet at the Woodruff Library and issued a statement condemning the verdict and requesting that the student leadership stay calm. The students were not to be deterred. Around mid-afternoon on Thursday, students gathered and resumed their protest. They met with Mayor Jackson on the steps of City Hall. Mayor Jackson misread the intensity of their anger and gave them no satisfaction with his remarks. On to Underground Atlanta, they threw bricks and overturned a car. Atlanta police were out in force by then, directing the students back to campus.

The crowd grew even more volatile as students were joined by non-student protesters from the community who went through the streets looting stores and smashing glass storefronts. The protesters reached the downtown area in several waves beginning at 2 p.m. and ending about 6 p.m. Dozens were arrested.

On Friday morning, the heavy police presence was evident. Angry students were kept on campus by a show of force of about 100 Atlanta police officers in riot gear. Some students grew agitated by the officers and the sound of helicopters overhead. The CAU board met without incident, but I told them that it was uncertain what might unfold in the afternoon.

A student-initiated protest march would turn destructive. Hundreds of students had gathered on the steps of the Woodruff Library for a peaceful protest. As the march left campus, others who weren't students joined in. By the time the group reached Northside Drive headed toward downtown Atlanta, it had grown to mob-like proportions, and things began to get out of hand.

The group was met by the Georgia National Guard and Atlanta police. They surrounded the Atlanta University Center campuses and forced the protesters back to the AUC through John Hope/University Homes and onto the CAU campus from the East. I left my office and saw firsthand how the National Guard and Atlanta Police were treating the students. It was violent, and in *my* view, unnecessary. Students were stunned by such a presence on their campus, their home. Repeatedly, I requested that the police presence be removed from the campus to give our public safety department the opportunity to bring order. My appeals to the mayor of Atlanta and the police chief were ignored. At one point in the afternoon, tear gas canisters were lobbed into CAU dormitories, quadrangles, administrative buildings as well as on the CAU and Morehouse campuses.

I returned to my office and contacted some board members and my colleague presidents and suggested we meet in President LeRoy Keith's office at Morehouse to determine what role, if any, we should play in helping to bring the confrontation to a speedy conclusion. Keith was the chair of the Council of Presidents at that time and we wanted to make sure that we were in accord on whatever actions we should take. We met in his office and observed the developments on television. We called Mayor Jackson and asked him to withdraw the police. By then, however, the situation had spiraled out of control. The number of protesters escalated, many of whom were not AUC students. The bookstore on the corner of Brawley and Fair was set on fire, and a liquor store located two blocks from the main campus was being looted, all of which was graphically displayed on television and broadcast locally and nationally.

It was sheer pandemonium. Students were crying. Police officers were beating students and forcing them to enter the Clark Atlanta dormitories, even though those who were part of the chaos came from all over the AUC campuses and from off-campus. Because the campus grounds are contiguous, persons unfamiliar with the AUC, even police officers and television commentators, could not distinguish one AUC campus from another. Police simply saw that students were congregating, and they were trying to disperse them. Student anger became progressively worse as long as the police presence continued.

"My reaction was first one of disbelief," said Carl Ware, then chairman of the Clark Atlanta University Board of Trustees. "Here we had Maynard Jackson, mayor of the city of Atlanta, and Eldrin Bell was police chief (both graduates of AUC schools). We have a black college campus with leadership, board of trustees, faculty, student body, and we all pretty much know each other. We were friends, members of the same community. And I felt that show of force was unnecessary, heavy-handed and terribly insensitive. Such an invasion of campus boundaries did not take place during the Civil Rights protests of the 1960s."

By Saturday, blame was settling. Students blamed everyone from the media to the mayor to the police for Friday's confrontation. Campus officials blamed Atlanta officials for their overreaction to initially peaceful student protests. Many blamed the media for coverage that characterized the violence as student-based, ignoring the high numbers of nonstudents who contributed to the chaos. I called a meeting of the student body to meet with them face to face to listen to their views and concerns. On Saturday night, I was interviewed on a local television station. Among other responses to their questions, I indicated that the police were not invited to come on our campus, should not have invaded any of the AUC campuses and their presence was not only unnecessary, but it was wrong.

Despite those and other challenges, overall the period was marked by our united focus at Clark Atlanta to keep moving forward.

CHAPTER 9

The Remarkable Rise of Clark Atlanta University

Merging cultures, streamlining operations, creating academic programs and combining faculties and staffs dominated the early years of Clark Atlanta University. But what really put the school on the academic map was its emergence as a research institution. "There is a real sense here that soon we are going to be able to compete with any other institution in the country for research dollars in a variety of fields," said C. Reynold Verret, an associate professor of chemistry at Clark Atlanta University, quoted in the 1995 *Chronicle of Higher Education* article, "The Remarkable Rise of Clark Atlanta University."

In 1994 alone, the University had won $35 million in federal science and engineering grants, nearly 12 times the amount Clark College and Atlanta University received combined in 1980. In 1992, Clark Atlanta University won more federal grants for science and engineering than any other Historically Black College. In that year, Clark Atlanta won $29 million in federal science and engineering grants.

A strategy for Clark Atlanta University had been created that had several elements. Most importantly, the University was proactive about seeking grants and making research a priority school by school. It also moved beyond grant competitions that were restricted to black colleges or institutions with large ethnic minority populations. In 1994, nearly half of the $35 million total came from grants for which any institution of higher education could compete. That year, Clark Atlanta received grants to study genetics (from the National Institutes of Health), new uses for plastics (from the Department of Energy and the Department of Defense) and environmental technologies (from the Environmental Protection Agency and the Department of Energy.

The University also focused on establishing the infrastructure needed to create a top-flight research institution. By 1992, the university had doubled its science faculty to 112 and doubled the number of students in science, engineering and math to 809 undergraduate and 161 graduate students. The department of engineering sciences was established and with a major grant from the Office of Naval Research, the PRISM-D Program was created that offered an accelerated program for undergraduate students through the doctorate education in the natural sciences and mathematics.

A number of research priorities were outlined, including computer science, materials research, molecular biology and environmental toxicology. A wide-range of interests was designed to give the school the ability to seek funds from a number of federal agencies—including the Department of Defense, the Department of Energy, the National Science Foundation, the National Institutes of Health and the Environmental Protection Agency—and protect itself from budget cuts or shifts in focus in any one agency.

Symbolic of the University's commitment to the sciences was the state-of-the-art research center which opened in 1995. First proposed when I was Chair of the Department of Chemistry in 1975 at Atlanta

University and then expanded in the early 1980s under the leadership of President Williams and Vice President Bota, the 200,000 square-foot building at the time provided more space than all of the academic and administrative space on the entire Atlanta University campus. The U.S. Department of Energy provided an initial planning grant of $500,000 with a commitment to provide the full funding for a $30 million facility.

After I became president of Clark College in March 1988, construction of the research facility was on track, but because of uncertainties in the language of the Congressional Records for the enabling legislation, only about half of this money had been appropriated. Following the consolidation of Clark College and Atlanta University, ground was broken for the Research Center in September 1989, with only half the funding in place. We took a calculated risk, and rather than downsize the scope of the building, a shell was constructed which remained empty for three years until Bota and I could secure the funding from private and federal sources to build out the balance of the structure as originally planned.

When the building was completed in 1995, it contained some of the best equipment available used daily to advance the research and teaching in the areas of science, mathematics, engineering and technology. Playing particularly important roles in addition to Williams and Bota were John Deutch, Institute Professor of Science at MIT and Former Secretary of Energy, Admiral James Watkins, who followed Deutch as Energy Secretary; numerous staff members in the Department of Energy, Congressman John Lewis, Senator Sam Nunn, the Woodruff Foundation; the Georgia Research Alliance; and the National Science Foundation.

Hand in hand with our commitment to science and research was a dedication to international studies. Atlanta University faculty and staff had long been involved in African and Caribbean programs since the early 1960s through programs like the Peace Corps and Fulbright Fellows. Clark Atlanta University inherited this emphasis on international relations from Atlanta University and enlarged it with academic, administrative and technical assistance.

It was the faculty, of course, who provided the academic leadership and stature to the new University that led to its growth and prestige. Some were extraordinarily gifted and aggressive in fulfilling the mission of teaching, research and service, appropriate to an emerging research institution. A complete listing of full-time faculty for the year, 1990-91, is provided in the Appendix.

About 10 percent of the University student body comprised international students, and the students, faculty and staff spoke more than 50 languages, according to Earle Clowney, Chair of the Department of Foreign Languages. In 1991, an Office of International Programs was established to help focus the University's efforts in five areas:

• Training and technical assistance
• Information and resource programs
• Student services
• Consortia and institutional linkages
• Research and non degree scholarly programs

Department programs included the Francophone Management Training Program, the Egyptian Child Survival Project, Haitian

Special Education Training Program, Togolese Women's Management Program, health management training programs and a special program with the United Nations Institute for Training and Research (UNITAR) that sponsored the Cecil Ram United Nations Semester Program that attracted students from around the world.

The University's international focus was greatly strengthened by several persons who came to the University with vast experience in international development work. Former Atlanta University professor Shelby Lewis returned as Associate Vice President for Research and Sponsored Programs and for research initiatives in the social sciences. Earl Picard, an alumnus of the University, joined the staff as Director of International Training.

The School of International Affairs was first proposed by Cecil Alexander during a meeting of the Board of Trustees when the discussions of consolidation began in 1988. Following a short planning process headed by James Jones, Professor of Public Administration, an international search was conducted that led to the appointment of Herschelle Challenor as first Dean of the School. Financial Support for the Office of International Training and Internationalization initiatives came from USAID and a major grant from the Kellogg Foundation. Clark Atlanta became a sister institution to the University of Thomasina in Madagascar and was the only university in the nation engaged in a partnership with the United Nations that offered students an academic U.N. Semester Program.

In addition, the University hosted a health management training program, and tripartite conference, "Women's Issues in the

Workplace," for women representing Training. In the 1990s, 10 countries, including India, Poland, Nicaragua, Mali and Jamaica, made visits to the University. The University also hosted numerous delegations from Benin, Brazil, Russia, China, Japan, France, Egypt, Ethiopia, Madagascar, Nigeria, South Africa, Congo, China, and Zimbabwe. Four CAU English department faculty took a 10-day study tour of Japanese universities to strengthen the interpretation of Japanese poetry and prose in the University's world literature courses. In 1995, the Southern Center for Studies in Public Policy under the leadership of Robert Holmes, Director of the Center who completed his doctoral work in Chinese Studies, hosted Asian and African-American scholars from the East-West Center for the "Challenges to Growth in Asia" Conference.

Clark Atlanta University was proving itself to be wide in mission and deep in its commitment to a community that stretched far beyond the boundaries of its campus. Since the 1970s, the School of Arts and Sciences housed an Africana Women's Studies Program which offered a program of study leading to the Master of Arts degree and the University awarded honorary degrees to several distinguished Africans, including Nelson Mandela, Desmond Tutu, Alhaji Adamu, Babacar Ndiaye and Nicephore Soglo when he was President of Benin. His excellency Dr. Adamu, served unofficially as the CAU Ambassador in Nigeria and later became the Nigerian Ambassador to the U. S. He commissioned the Benin bronze sculpture titled "Communication Linkages" that is located on the Thayer Hall Quadrangle celebrating the global link between Africa and African Americans.

A natural balance to our commitment to science and research was a commitment to the social sciences and to the arts. As First

Lady of Clark Atlanta, Brenda, helped lead that effort through the creation of the Clark Atlanta University Guild. With the help of the Office of Development and support of key alumni and members of the community, the Guild was created in 1992. Within two years, contributions from local businesses provided a four-year tuition scholarship totaling $40,000 to the first Guild scholar, for the 1993-94 academic year. In following years, smaller scholarships were added, and money was restricted to begin building an endowment.

The Guild created popular fund-raisers that featured performers of the day. The first fund-raising event was "An Evening of Shakespeare" with actor Charles "Roc" Dutton, in 1995, which involved the campus theater group, the CAU Players, and musical groups. Later came "Jazz Under the Stars," which featured nationally known musicians such as Nancy Wilson, Jeffrey Osborne, Roberta Flack, Roy Ayres, James Moody, Regina Belle, and Gerald Albright and Wynton Marsalis. Over this time, the CAU Guild raised more than $1 million and provided financial support for 176 students. The Guild Scholarship provided a great opportunity to help talented young people perform, get an education, and promote the university.

Besides the strong internal focus on academics and the arts, Clark Atlanta University was also taking its place as a citizen of what was about to be a city decked out for the world. The 1996 Olympics contributed significantly to much of the physical change that took place on campus

The early 1990s in Atlanta were primarily about building and looking ahead to the future. It was true for the city, and it was true for Clark Atlanta University. A foundation was laid, transformation was under way and there was true energy in the air. Even the reaffirmation of accreditation in 1995 came with special precedent. Under the direction of Bettye Clark and a Steering Committee co-chaired by Clark and Edward Davis, the University was reaffirmed with no follow-up reports required.

The 1996 Olympics jump-started much of the physical change that took place both on campus and throughout the city and state. With Clark Atlanta, it was also a natural evolution of a young institution finding its balance and becoming a community member that gives back, a destination for world and national leaders and a self-sufficient organization managing millions of dollars a year. Externally, the Olympics symbolized growth and change. Internally, establishing a system to manage the school's finances symbolized Clark Atlanta's growth and maturity. Academically, CAU made a major contribution to the Games by serving as the Host Broadcast Training Program (HBTP) that trained more than 1200 students from schools in Georgia and throughout the United States. The HBPT was coordinated by Gloria James in collaboration with the Atlanta Committee for the Olympic Games.

From 1989–2002, almost $150 million was spent on construction and renovation of existing facilities, which helped increase the value of Clark Atlanta University's assets from $63 million in 1989 to $215 million. Funds were received from the Atlanta Organizing Committee for the 1996 Olympics, from the State of Georgia through the Georgia Research Alliance and major contributions were received from the U. S. Department of Education (through Title III), the United Methodist

Church, the Coca-Cola Company and the Kresge, Ford, Mott, Kellogg and Knight Foundations.

In 2002, an additional $7 million in gifts from the Woodruff and Campbell Foundations, which with several smaller donations provided the major share of the new academic center constructed in 2004. The Center was later named the Carl and Mary Ware Academic Center in recognition of a $2 million gift to the University that kicked off the 1997 Capital Campaign. The second largest individual gift to the University was $1 million given in 2002 by Mr. David Luke III, John Luke Jr., and Douglas Luke of the MeadWestvaco Company.

By the time the Olympic Games began in Summer 1996, changes on Clark Atlanta's campus included:

- A $17 million dormitory at James P. Brawley Drive and Beckwith Streets. Financed by revenue bonds. It housed the international press during the Games and featured 470 single-occupancy rooms sectioned into two—and three-room suites wired for Internet access.
- The Atlanta University Center Pedestrian Promenade. Funded by the Metro Atlanta Olympic Games Authority (MAOGA), it served as a walkway intended to connect the Vine City MARTA station to the West End station by passing through the AUC and CAU campus;
- The Olympic field hockey venue, paid for by the AOC, a 5,000-seat stadium later used as the primary venue for the Special Olympics soccer field and then as a rehearsal room for the 100-piece Marching Panther Band and as a football stadium

with locker rooms for the University; The track was six lanes which were part of the Olympic track during the 1966 Games.

- The exterior of the Student Center paid for by University bond proceeds and named for Bishop Cornelius Henderson.;
- A new 500-car parking deck, paid for by bond proceeds;
- Renovation of the Trevor Arnett Hall reading room to accommodate a new art gallery to house the University's internationally known African-American art collection, paid for with private funding totaling $2.5 million.
- A new entrance to the campus at Martin Luther King Jr., Dr, where a small replica of Harkness Hall denoted the new official entrance and welcome center paid for by MAOGA.

The initial planning for the construction of the first and second pitch field hockey venues for the Olympics called for two identical 10,000-seat stadia for Clark Atlanta and also for Morris Brown, across the street from each other. This did not make sense to me and Raymond Williams, the CAU Athletic Director, nor did it make sense to Calvert Smith, then president of Morris Brown. With the active and enthusiastic support of the athletic directors from both institutions, several key trustees and alumni, we proposed instead to merge our athletic programs and take advantage of the tremendous opportunity afforded by the Olympics: construct one major (15,000-seat) football stadium and a smaller stadium (5,000 seat) for track and field that would serve both institutions. We agreed in principle and advised the Olympic planning committee to do so. We also developed a blueprint for the combination of the two athletic programs in 1994. Unfortunately, following the Olympics, President Smith left Morris Brown. The agreement was not honored by his successors.

The key contributors to the influence of the Olympics on the physical infrastructure and development of the campus were Billy Payne, Andrew Young, Shirley Franklin and A. D. Frazier. Their consistent commitment to support the development of Olympic venues in the Atlanta University Center played a significant role in providing more than $50 million in infrastructure support to be used during the Games and afterwards by the individual campuses. The football stadium, softball field, track, and tennis courts at CAU are major parts of that legacy, which greatly enhanced the University's intercollegiate and intramural athletics programs. Prior to 1996, the University used off-site venues for football and baseball games, tennis and track and field events.

The University had a long history of varsity and intramural sporting activities dating from 1913 as a member of the Southern Intercollegiate Athletic Conference (SIAC). Since 1988, Clark Atlanta University has produced excellent players in each sport that it sponsors—football, basketball, track and field, tennis golf, swimming, cross-county running, volleyball, softball and cheerleading. The University is a member of Division II, National Collegiate Athletic Association (NCAA) Numerous SIAC divisional championships help attest to the strength of the University's athletic programs and the leadership and success of a dedicated coaching staff. For the first time in the University's history, all of the sports facilities were located on campus.

References

Stephen Beard, "The Remarkable Rise of Clark Atlanta University," *The Chronicle of Higher Education.* March 24, 1995.
Clark Atlanta University Magazine, 1966 Commemorative Issue.

President Clinton visits CAU

Check presentation by Dept of Energy, 1992

CHAPTER 10

Coming of Age

Ending the year with a balanced budget and an unqualified audit are a constant worry for public and private institutions alike. In each year, Clark Atlanta University concluded the year with a balanced budget and an unqualified audit opinion. This was a non negotiable item for the CFO, the Board and for me. That does not mean there were not challenging years—two of 12 years were more financially challenging than others.

The first challenging year was 1995, following the attempt at implementation of the JD Edwards software system that would facilitate grant and contract reporting without proper activation of the purchasing module. The University avoided a potential deficit of $4 million that year because of the availability of unrestricted financial reserves from several accounts and the application of the new accounting rule, FAS 116, which allowed the University to book pledges from the UNCF Capital Campaign and other donors.

The second most difficult year was 1997 when the U.S. Dept. of Education placed Clark Atlanta's Office of Student Financial Aid on reimbursement status because of inadequate administration of Title IV funds. The University's fiscal operations improved following this period. The crisis prompted the University to re-staff the financial aid office and appoint new leadership. The reporting structure for the office was shifted from Student Affairs to Fiscal Affairs. At that time, Charles Teamer, and alumnus who has just recently retired from distinguished careers as Vice President for Finance at Wiley College and Dillard University was appointed CFO. He helped stabilize the financial condition of the University and led the institution through a re-examination of its policies and relationships between fiscal affairs, academic affairs and financial aid through a series of workshops called Institutional Effectiveness, which improved the university's handling of Title IV Funds.

After two years of intensive work, the U.S. Dept. of Education removed Clark Atlanta from reimbursement status and recognized the University as an exemplary institution in the administration of student financial aid. Major kudos for this accomplishment go to Teamer and to his successor, George Ross. Ross formed a great team with Joel Harrell, Vice President for Student Affairs and collectively, they and their staffs made major contributions to this rapid response by implementing the needed infrastructure to bring the basic financial operations of the university to the level required for more efficient management of Title IV funds.

There was one additional complication to the University's financial operations. During the largest budget year (1996-1997), about 50 percent of the $122 million operating budget came from the federal government for research grants or infrastructure and program support. There were several very large grants in excess of $5 million per year—USAID, the Egyptian Child Survival Project and projects for international training, Head Start and Title III, which had a large matching component. Other income came from several NSF, NASA and NIH research and infrastructure grants in excess of $1 million per year, one large pass-through grant (DOE Consortium

Grant) and over 50 smaller grants of less than $1 million per year. There were also several smaller grants, which were financed based on advanced payment, and there were federal funds from Title IV. Student Financial Aid totaled almost $50 million in loans and grants. The largest single private gifts were primarily the annual funding from the United Negro College Fund and the United Methodist Church of approximately $1 million each per year and the Kellogg and Woodruff Foundations, which provided one-time gifts in excess of $1 million per year.

It was a challenge to create the internal infrastructure and controls to oversee the management of such a large volume of grants, contracts and gifts with the appropriate timely reporting required for so many federal and private agencies on so many federal grants and private gifts. In 1995, the University separated from the computer operations housed by The Atlanta University Center, Inc., and invested considerable financial resources in a new computer system to help address the massive reporting grants/contracts accounting and reporting requirements to handle grants and contracts management at the level needed for the university.

Two new offices were staffed to handle the post—and pre-award financial and program, reporting needs required by the federal government. The sheer volume of federal grants and contracts required draw-downs of approximately $5 million per month and involved six of the largest federal agencies, each with different reporting guidelines.

By 1993, the University was receiving almost 12,000 first-year applications for admissions. Most requested on-campus housing. At that time, the University had only 1,350 beds on campus, far fewer than student demand. For three years, the University attempted to accommodate this demand with a variety of short-term arrangements with local motels and hotels. Students loved the arrangements, because, in general, when a motel was used, they would have private bathrooms, air-conditioning and television. However, the University elected not to renew the housing arrangement in favor of construction of more permanent resident halls on campus.

In 1998, the University had grown to an enrollment of almost 5,800 (nearly achieving the 2010 goal of 6,000) with an operating budget in excess of $100 million per year. The endowment grew from $16 million at the time of the consolidation in 1988 to $32 million in 1997.

It was clear at the beginning of the consolidation that reliance on endowment and tuition and fee increases alone would be inadequate to provide a revenue base for program development and enhancement and to overcome the cash deficit in the short term. Major external fund-raising would be essential to fuel the growth and development of the new University.

The strategy was to approach fund-raising using three complementary components. The first component was to capitalize on the new University's favorable reputation with the federal government because of its expanded capacity to engage in research/ contract work. Such funding would serve as a source of support for infrastructure and program development in areas, such as physical sciences, engineering and education. The second component was designed to address support for other program areas, like social work, business, humanities, social sciences and international affairs, from the private sector. The third component was to use low-interest, revenue-bond financing for major capital projects such as residence halls, which would have an independent revenue stream to handle the debt service.

In 1988, Clark Atlanta borrowed $1 million from a local bank for funds to renovate the E. L. Simon Courts. Later that year, a low-interest loan was secured from the federal government to renovate Haven-Warren Hall. The decisions to acquire long-term debt for capital projects was a conscious decision made by the board because there were two built-in reserve accounts to handle any short-term limitation on cash to repay the loan and for capital improvements, and revenue streams from the increase in student enrollment and occupancy in student housing that would handle the debt service.

The University went to the bond market three times. The first was in 1989 for $5 million to provide the matching needed to secure the loan from the federal government that had been made available to Atlanta University in 1986 for renovation of Ware and Bumstead Halls. That loan would have expired if the necessary matching conditions had not been met. The University was a new entity in the bond market and these bonds were just above investment grade. The second approach to the bond market was in 1993 to refinance and defease the 1989 bonds to get an improved rate and additional funding of $10 million to construct a Student Center and parking deck. The University received extraordinary assistance in responding to these financial transactions from an external consultants, Harold

Sims and James Brown and Associated, who were committed to assisting HBCUs negotiate the complicated bond markets.

The 1993 bonds were not only investment grade but given the growth and potential of the University were rated by Moody's as Baa, the first time ever the University was rated as such. The third bond issue was 1995 when the 1993 bonds were defeased and the issue was increased to accommodate the construction of a $17 million residence hall.

Audits for the two years ending 1994 and 1995, less than six years after the consolidation, show the volume of federal grants/contracts at about $55 million and indirect cost recovery of $3.7 million. By 1995, the research center for science and education was completed at an initial cost of $32 million. In addition, eight buildings (Haven-Warren, Knowles, Oglethorpe, Sage-Bacote, Trevor Arnett, Brawley, Ware and Bumstead Halls) were renovated, a new dormitory and parking deck had been built, the University acquired Park Street Church as a gift from the United Methodist Church, North Georgia Conference, all the houses on faculty row were renovated and occupied, and major construction was under way to make the campus ready for the 1996 Olympics with a stadium, new residence hall and air-conditioning of Brawley, Merner, Holmes and Pfeiffer halls.

During the 1994-1995 year, private gifts and grants totaled $14.4 million, the largest of which was a $3 million gift from the Kellogg Foundation to support the creation of the School of International Affairs and Development. The University also completed successfully its First Capital Campaign, raising $10.5 million from the private sector. The University's growth was also being recognized nationally and described in The Chronicle of Higher Education, *"The Remarkable Rise of Clark Atlanta University."*

Clark Atlanta University had been on a course of rapid growth and development toward becoming more competitive with peer institutions in terms of salaries, benefits, scholarships, and academic support for faculty and staff. In 1997, however, federal sector support experienced earlier in the decade had waned and there were no immediate prospects for a return to that early level of federal funding. Consequently, the University began downsizing those aspects of its operation that depended on federal funds.

The Egyptian Child Survival Project had ended after two extensions (USAID policy precluded additional extension), and the Head Start Program and most of the activities in International Training were discontinued. Elimination of these programs alone resulted in an overall annual budget and staff reduction of about $15 million and 150 persons. For the children enrolled in the Head Start Program, guaranteed admission to the University with a tuition scholarship was extended for those who performed well academically through high school and applied for admission and met the University's admission criteria.

The University also started a comprehensive analysis of its overall staffing pattern and began strategic reductions of personnel in its unrestricted operations. As a consequence, enrollment was curtailed and program expansion was discontinued unless such expansion could be justified by new sources of revenue for long-term support. Under the leadership of Provost Sherman Jones and subsequently Provost Winfred Harris, a new strategic academic plan was developed that identified academic areas for strengthening or elimination. By 1999, the total operating budget had been reduced to just over $100 million from a high of $122 million in 1997. Further strategic reductions continued for the next several years to assure that personnel levels were in line with the University's capacity to retain a quality academic graduate and undergraduate program, an enrollment of at least 5,000 students, a faculty/student ratio of approximately 16:1 and a balanced operating budget that also satisfied the 1995 bond covenants.

By the end of the 2002 fiscal year, the University was in its best financial position since the consolidation and improving under George Ross' leadership in fiscal affairs. Bond holders expressed increased confidence in him and the University fiscal operations and maintained the bond rating at Baa. Since 1988, more than $570 million had been invested in the University to support academic programs, research and public service activities, infrastructure enhancements, and new and renovated facilities. Of this amount, almost $150 million was applied to new construction and renovated facilities (See Appendix).

Mandela Convocation

Wynton Marsalis at CAU commencement 2001

CHAPTER 11
Unlimited Possibilities

Most of the major events and highlights that occurred during the period 1989-2002 are chronicled in 24 issues of the Clark Atlanta University Magazine. Toni Mosley was the editor-in-chief for most of those years. The last in the series was written by Catherine LeBlanc, Former Executive Director of the White House Initiative on HBCUs in collaboration with Getchel Caldwell and titled "Unlimited Possibilities." My final Commencement address in May 2002 had the same title. Compared to the excitement that greeted each new academic year, the periodic challenges were minor. There were few surprises, and most of them were handled by the staff without fanfare. Occasionally, an article appeared in the local papers about "problems" at the University, but most of them could be characterized as growing pains, and were addressed quickly. The University's public relations staff had a good relationship with the local newspapers and television stations.

The first ten years were characterized by numerous special events that brought visibility and prestige to the University and helped establish it as one of the places to be in higher education in the 1990s. Among them were visits and convocations celebrating the contributions and lives of Nelson Mandela, Bishop Desmond Tutu, former President Jimmy Carter, President William J. Clinton, William Gates, William Gray, Ambassador Andrew Young, Leon Sullivan, General Colin Powell, Mae Jemison, Johnnie Cochran, Vice President and Mrs. Al Gore, Pele', Henry Aaron, Billye Aaron, the

Reverend Joseph Lowery, Quincy Jones, Vernon Jordan, John Lewis, Alexis Herman, Wynton Marsalis, Lou Rawls, Clifton Wharton, Ann Fudge, Bebe Moore, Nikki Giovanni, Danny Glover, Betty Shabazz, Ossie Davis, Ruby Dee, Hugh Price, Terry McMillan and Kenneth Chenault, to name a few.

Other special events include the following:

- Clark Atlanta joins with five other universities in Georgia to create the Georgia Research Alliance.
- The School of Business celebrated its 45th Anniversary.
- The School of Library and Information Sciences celebrated its 50th anniversary.
- The women's tennis team finished first in the SIAC.
- University inherits a 22-acre estate from the bequest from alumna Lucy Rucker Aiken.
- Following a total renovation of Dean Sage Hall, the building was renamed Sage-Bacote Hall in honor of Clarence A. Bacote.
- Clark Atlanta's Environmental Justice Resource Center receives international attention as it expands its initiatives include studies and workshops in South Africa. Began in 1994 by Dr. Robert Bullard, Ware Professor of Sociology and Director of the Center, is recognized as a leading international authority on environmental issues affecting people of color.

In 1994, Tina Dunkley returned to the University as head of the historic Waddell Gallery which had been relegated to the basement of Trevor Arnett Hall. A $2 million renovation of the former reading room of Trevor Arnett Library for new gallery space and restoration of the Hale Woodruff murals in the foyer under her leadership offered major improvements and a more fitting space for the extraordinary collection. In 2000, many of the works which had been with Atlanta University since the 1940s were conserved as part of a touring exhibit, "To Conserve a Legacy: American Art from Historically Black Colleges and Universities." This exhibit included works from five other HBCUs.

By 2001, just over a decade after consolidation, the University had achieved recognition as one of the top 200 regional universities in the United States. It was ranked nationally in yearly reviews of America's best colleges and universities in magazines such as *U. S. News and World Report, Black Issues in Higher Education, Black Enterprise* and *Money* Magazine. The University ranked among the top five in areas where the doctorate was offered and number one in the awarding of Ph.D. degrees to African Americans in political science.

Beyond legacy, vision and global outreach, faculty and staff played a critical role in setting the tone and standards for the new university. Their dedication and distinguished service were responsible for the University's moving from tier 4 to tier 3 in the *U. S. News and World Report* listing for national universities (four years ahead of schedule!) and becoming the only historically black private university listed as a Doctoral/Research-Intensive institution in the Carnegie Classification of U. S. colleges and universities. Interdisciplinary research institutes and centers were created with new external funding to engage students and faculty in a wide range of research, teaching and service activities. They included:

- Army Center of Excellence in Electronic Sensors and Combat
- Army Center for Research in Information Sciences
- Center for Excellence in Microelectronics and Photonics
- Center for Surface Chemistry and Catalysis
- Center for Theoretical Studies of Physical Systems
- Distance Learning Instructional Technology Education Center
- Earth Systems Science Program
- Environmental Justice Research Center
- High Performance Polymers and Composites Center
- Joseph E. Lowery Institute for Justice and Human Rights
- W. E. B. DuBois Institute
- Web Technology Development and Training Center

These were added to the following centers and institutes which were in place prior to the consolidation:

- National Institutes of Health Research Center in Minority Institutions
- Resource Center for Science and Engineering
- Southern Center for Studies in Public Policy

The School of Library and Information Studies continued as the only accredited School of Library Science in the state of Georgia and Clark Atlanta University faculty and students distinguished themselves in several national competitions. The University's teams took first place in both the 2001 Honda Campus All-Star Academic Quiz Bowl and the 2001 Wearable Computer Design Competition of the Fifth International Symposium on Wearable Computers. And through initiatives such as the BS/MST Program in Mathematics Education, the BS/MBA in Accounting and Finance and the

Program for Research Integration and Support for Matriculation to the Doctorate (PRISM-D), capable students were provided the financial assistance to get both the bachelor's and master's degrees in five years. Additional student achievements included 5-time invited performances of the CAU Jazz Orchestra (James Patterson, Director) to the Montreux Jazz Festival (more times than any other college jazz orchestra) and the appearance of the Philharmonic Society at the Olympics in 1996, as backup for Gladys Knight and for Natalie Cole and a performance at Carnegie Hall (Glynn Halsey, Director). The Philharmonic Society was also featured in a CD with noted opera diva, Denyce Graves.

In October 2001, a team of five engineering and computer science students competed nationally and won the prestigious Grand Prize in the Fifth Annual International Symposium on Wearable Computers. The talented men and women that comprise the Philharmonic Society appeared at Carnegie Hall on November 2, 2001 with several other choirs for the World Premier Performance of "The Nativity" written by African-American composer, Earnestine Rogers Robinson. Additionally, the Panther Marching Band hosted the "World's Largest Band" during the 2001 summer band camp with more than 1,000 high school students participating from the metro Atlanta area. As a result, Clark Atlanta University was selected as the institutional site for the upcoming Century 2000 film, "Drumliine."

The University's commitment to identify and cultivate potential scholars was also evidenced by programs that targeted middle— and high-school students and their teachers. Examples include the Upward Bound Mathematics and Science Program, Workshops for High School Teachers, the nationally recognized Saturday Science

Academy, introduced in 1977 as a component of the Atlanta Resource Center and the Academic Preseason Program, a six-week summer experience for prospective college freshmen.

In 1998, the University created the CAU Press, with Charles Duncan as Editor, and resurrected publication of *PHYLON, A Review of Race and Culture,* widely recognized for more than 50 years as a source of significant African-American scholarly work, founded by W. E. B. DuBois in 1940 when he was a member of the faculty at Atlanta University.

The intellectual development of students was also enhanced by programs like the 32 year-old Writers Workshop Conference, the Julius C. Daugherty Endowed Lectureship Series in Law and Government initiated by a generous gift from his widow, Mrs. Thomasina Daugherty, the C. Eric Lincoln Lectureship Series, and the Dean's Executive Lecture Series at the School of Business, which exposed students and faculty to outstanding achievers and intellectuals in addition to the full time faculty.

Clark Atlanta University was built on the academic legacies of two great parents. The University has unlimited possibilities to continue growth and development in teaching, research, and service. By July 2002, at the time of my retirement as President, CAU had surpassed the benchmarks outlined in 1988 in the document, "Charting a Bold New Future."

Billye Aaron and Andy Young preside at Farewell Gala 2002

Dedication of Thomas W. Cole, Jr. Building 2002

APPENDIX I

Inaugural Address
Thomas W. Cole, Jr., President
September 24, 1989

Chairman Ware, Vice-Chairman Cordy, members of the Board of Trustees; presidents and colleagues from the Atlanta University Center; Chancellor Merideth, distinguished presidents and delegates from the colleges and universities from the United Methodist Church, and from learned societies and other professional organizations; elected officials; members of the faculty and staff, students, alumni and friends of Clark Atlanta University—thank you for your warm greetings and for your presence today on this special occasion. To everyone who participated in the inaugural celebration this past week—individuals and members of committees—and to those individuals who worked so hard as members of the inaugural steering committee to make this week memorable for me and the University, I offer my heartfelt thanks.

I am honored and humbled to stand before you today at this solemn investiture. I take seriously the magnitude, the urgency and the uniqueness that this occasion represents. I hold the gauntlet of leadership firmly with both hands. I hold it with reverence and humility. I hold it not as a possession, but as a gift from all of you who, in different ways, brought Clark Atlanta University into existence. For leadership is not something one has a right to have. Rather, it is a gift one must earn the right to receive.

During my tenure as president of Clark Atlanta University, I will work passionately for our institution. This is an enormous task, and I will not always be right. I ask for your best efforts, understanding and prayers so that I can do the job you have chosen me to so as if no one could do it better.

Today's occasion, embellished with pomp and circumstance and the melodious music of this special inaugural choir, is more than an inauguration. It is a christening, for a child is born in our academic center. We have watched it breathe long enough to know that its vital signs are good, and so there is promise of continued life, and the certainty of growth.

And we thank God for this opportunity at this time in this place to be participants together in this bold new venture.

This was no unwanted birth that followed an accidental conception. It was a planned conception in which two distinctive institutions willingly and enthusiastically participated as equal partners—as strong parents, each with an individual identity and an outstanding history, as a unique graduate school exclusively and as a liberal arts college. Just as a child carries the genes and characteristics of both parents, the new institution will carry the distinctive strengths of the parent institutions. And so the parents—Atlanta University and Clark College—have reason on *this day* to be proud of what they have created. Just as a child takes what it receives from both parents and makes its way to vistas the parents never knew, but desired for their own, so is this new institution, Clark Atlanta University, finding its own vistas. And thus, Atlanta University and Clark College have reason to look with pride to a future of promise, distinction and achievement for the institution that came from them.

On July 1, 1988, Clark Atlanta University was born, kicking, with a sense of urgency to become a world-class institution in the center, in the City of Atlanta, in the nation, indeed on this planet—a world-class institution born twelve years before the 21st Century to be a leader in the 21st Century. The birth was *on time and in time.*

During these past days of celebration, I have had many occasions to reflect on our past and to think about our future. I have reflected on the past presidents who led each of these institutions to their distinctive positions on the academic scene long before I arrived— two of them are with us today—Dr. Thomas D. Jarrett and Dr. Elias Blake; and on contributions of the faculty and alumni and the rich legacy they have left us. I am convinced that we are prepared for the challenge ahead, thanks to those who created our past and to the many of you who have inherited it. I know that I am not alone; and with the help of God and all of those inspired by our histories, we can move forward into our future.

And what do we envision for Clark Atlanta University? What new frontiers do we establish for ourselves? What is our role in the landscape of American higher education? In short, what is our mission?

Clark Atlanta University was born to seize the day. Carpe diem. Seize the day to make it an eternity of achievement.

Seize the day because we live in a world in which there is a sense or urgency for achievement—a sense of urgency for service and change as a persistent drumbeat for those who would stand up and be counted. It is not a distant drumbeat. It is close to home because the problems it calls attention to are neon signs in our communities and out nation.

In virtually all elements of American society—health, education, income and employment—the progress of minority groups has stalled. We are not educating our children adequately at a time when we will be increasingly dependent on the contributions of minorities and women in the labor force in the 21st century.

The trends are unmistakable. African Americans are losing ground in all indicators of educational achievement from grade school to graduate school. We are losing ground in the number of bachelor's, master's and doctorate degrees awarded; and in the production of teachers for our nation's public schools and faculty for our colleges and universities. We are producing fewer black scientists, mathematicians and engineers than we did twenty years ago.

As America prepares to enter its third century, this country is challenges as never before to maintain its competitive position in the global marketplace, to sustain the standard of living, to close the gap that separates minorities from the rest of America, and to bequeath to the next generation a more just order than their parents inherited.

As a nation, we have an enormous challenge before us. Despite more than two decades of equal opportunity and affirmative action, we not yet conquered the issues of access, equality and diversity in American higher education.

At Clark Atlanta University, we have a marvelous opportunity to restructure the university to address these challenges. We can not be all things to all people, and we will not try to be. We will concentrate on those program areas where we have historical strength undergirded by a strong liberal arts tradition, and emphasis in graduate and professional education in selected areas in the arts and sciences, business administration, education, library and information sciences and social work. But in all things we do, we will conform to the highest standards of excellence and performance—in the arts, humanities and sciences, in mass communications; in the quality of our facilities, and yes, in athletics.

As a nation, we have yet to discover the intellectual excitement and pragmatic value of a genuine commitment to explore the many ways in which the impact of the African American experience might affect our world view, our way of thinking about our problems and values. We want our students and faculty to demonstrate to the academic communities of the world the values of the black experience in creating our own art forms and literature, but also, in affecting the very way the communities of scholars and literate peoples think about literature and art forms.

In all disciplines and in all of the graduate and professional schools, there will be an infusion of scholarship on race, gender and class not typically found in American higher education. We cannot ignore women's issues, to do so would be tantamount to ignoring the reality of half of the people on this planet. We can not ignore or dismiss race; to do so would be to minimize the pervasive presence of race in all issues affecting the life and work in this country.

In the social sciences, we want to develop a strong corps of professionals who will use their talents to address the problems of the poor and deprived in this nation, because we ourselves are part of that heritage. We want to produce lawmakers who will consider the communities they serve more than themselves or political or economic gain. Our students must remind the world that values are important and there is a right and a wrong; and sometimes these are matters of the heart and compassion as much as they are of the heart and objective science. The new social science must blend the head and the heart, and our faculty must show us the way.

Our natural science programs must add our students to the numbers of those who take delight in discovery and creativity. But we must also add to the numbers of those who turn their skills to the great problems that face us as a nation and a people.

As we plan for the immediate future, there are six areas on which we will focus our attention:

- Teacher Education. We will contribute to the improvement of the nation's public schools by providing more and better trained teachers and principals through our school of education—men and women who believe that genius and talent are not bound by color or economic class. We need more teachers in all fields, especially in the sciences and mathematics, and we must prepare them better with more emphasis on content. We will offer scholarships and other incentives to encourage more students to choose teaching as a profession and we will serve as an important voice in restructuring American schools.

- Public and International Affairs. For almost a year, a task force has been working actively to develop the curriculum and program directions for a new school of public and international affairs; to produce more African American foreign service personnel and to provide training and technical assistance to elected public officials; to coordinate all of the many individual educational and training programs in the international arena now at the University, and to infuse an international dimension in the curriculum across the board the help prepare our students for leadership in a global society. Our students must develop an understanding of the geopolitical orientations, the cultures, economies, and religions of people around the world.

- We will produce more black librarians, MBA's and Master's and Doctorates in critical areas through our graduate and professional schools. We need more African American professionals in all areas. We will strengthen our capacity in selected graduate programs and increase access to other programs in areas through cooperative academic program arrangements at the graduate level with other universities. We will look at joint opportunities across the board, but particularly, in the natural mathematical and computer sciences and engineering, where minority underrepresentation is especially critical.

- We will encourage minority entrepreneurship through our School of Business, and serve minority entrepreneurs on a continuing basis with technical assistance and management skills that will help minority businesses survive and prosper.

- We will place a major emphasis on community development and public service focused on the so-called underclass and social issues confronting our community through our School of Social Work. Division between town and gown is antithetical to the mission of Clark Atlanta University. Clearly, our location obligates us and our mission compels us to be concerned about change in the immediate as well as the larger community. We have established a Community Development Corporation already that will assist in harnessing resources from the University, city and state and from the private sector. In cooperation with our sister institutions in the Atlanta University Center, we will improve the quality of housing on our immediate community as well as provide needed social services to the residents who are our nearest neighbor.

- And finally, we will give attention to the undergraduate curriculum and the quality of student life for undergraduate and graduate students. It is important that our undergraduate students receive a broad-based, value-centered education, not a hodgepodge of courses, grade requirements and credits. There should be something special that should differentiate an institution with a historical relationship to the Methodist Church from institutions that offer only a broad-based undergraduate curriculum, something special that incorporates ethics and moral values in the undergraduate experience. We must teach out students more than facts and skills. We must also teach them in an environment of integrity that demonstrates that we care for them and that they succeed.

Although Clark Atlanta University is just a year old, because of the legacy of its parents we already have moved from crawling to walking. Before we heard the starter's gun, we were "on our mark," ready to start sprinting and making new records. We will run hard and fast, but we know we will never reach the finish line, for there is no end to the race for access, equality and service.

And we will run *with*, not against our partners in the Atlanta University Center, clearing hurdles with them, not putting hurdles in their path. As we run, we will be saying to ourselves again and again, *carpe diem—aprovecha el momento*—seize the day.

We will not be in competition with any institution. Rather, we will be in competition with the conditions that prevent our people from taking charge of their destinies, circumstances that lower their self-esteem, despair that robs dreamers of belief in dreams, mediocrity that puts poorly prepared people in influential positions. We will be in competition with self-doubt, apathy, despair, and devotion to material success rather than service to others. If together we do not run faster than social, economic, educational and spiritual ills, they will win and *all* of us will lose.

When people said before our birth, "It can't be done," we heard them, but turned our ear to the voices of the believers who said, "*Carpe diem—lee yung shee-en zi-du chin kwahng—seize the day.*

When people said on July 1, 1988, "It has been done, but it will not succeed." We heard them, but we turned our ears to the voices of those who said, "dawns are not new among our people, *"Carpe diem—iwappnia, njia hupratikana—seize the day.*

Seize the day and build Clark Atlanta University into a world-class university that will endure as the pyramids and the sphinx. All of us in our individual ways must seize the day for Clark Atlanta University.

Trustees, you were in a sense midwives in the process that brought forth Clark Atlanta University. Unlike traditional midwives who leave once the sounds of life are strong, you must continue to work. Indeed, more than ever, your guidance and support—your knowing hands—are needed, for being born is not half as demanding as staying alive and remaining strong. I say to you, "Carpe Diem—seize the day."

I say *Carpe Diem* in an even more compelling voice to the alumni of the two original institutions, for you have what is perhaps the most challenging task of all—to create a new identity for yourselves while keeping sacred memories of your years at your alma mater, to develop loyalty to a new institution that the strengths of your alma mater made possible. I say to you, "Carpe Diem—wir mussen die Gelegenheit ergreifen—seize the day."

Faculty teach, students learn. It is the staff that serves in all areas of the running of a university. Your expertise is the axis on which registration, graduation exercises, class schedules, room assignments, trustee meetings, faculty grants, and other essentials turn so smoothly. Your attention to details keeps the lights on, the grounds clean, the food nutritious. Your professionalism and love for the university will keep alumni, parents, students, the faculty and the president informed and happy. You are vital and you must take pride in what you give to the university. In the years ahead, like all of us, you must give more. I say to the staff, *"Carpe Diem—profite-toi du jour—seize the day."*

To the faculty, I say "{Hold firm in your hands the magic wand of motivation, stimulation, challenge and scholarship." In a sense, we will run the marathon as winners only if you are either the runners of the trainers who are teaching the new runners how to clear hurdles without dropping the baton. What you do with the people we serve—our students—is the contribution that makes all achievements of the university possible. You should be scholars conducting research and writing the books, but above all, you must be teachers, teaching future scholars who will write books, conduct research, who will lead and make a difference. I say to you. *"Carpe Diem—ko no hi no, kou ki o ri you su ru—seize the day."*

I make you, our students, last, only to emphasize that you are first in our mission. Your task is the most difficult and the most important. To a world in chaos, you must bring order by putting your studies first. In a world of glitter, you must shine and dazzle, by putting your studies first. At a time when our people are losing ground, you must regain the ground and surpass it by putting your studies first. You must seize every opportunity we give you for excellence, and even create opportunities we might not give. The world waits for you to seize the day and become the leaders of the 21st century.

Carpe diem—iwaponia, njia hupratikana—aprovecha el momento—profite-toi du jour—seize the day.

I accept the challenge of leadership that has been passed on to me. I am optimistic about our future because our past serves as prolog and a mighty resource and foundation for this university. We are well-positioned for the 21st century and I call on all of you—this great and good community of students, scholars, researchers, staff and friends—to join me as we chart a bold new future for Clark Atlanta University.

Thank you very much.

CLARK ATLANTA UNIVERSITY

ADMINISTRATIVE OFFICERS (1990-1992)

Office of the President
  Thomas W. Cole, Jr., Ph.D., President
  Gloria P. James, Ph.D., Executive Assistant to the President
  Michael A. Baskin, J. D., General Counsel
  Carl Spight, Ph.D., Special Assistant (1990-1991)
  Om Puri, Ph.D., Special Assistant
Office of the Provost
  Conrad Snowden, Ph.D., Provost (1989-1990)
  Charles Churchwell, Ph.D., Interim Provost (1990-1993)
  Nathaniel Pollard, Ph.D., Associate Provost
  Debra McCurdy, Ph.D., Assistant Provost
  Lou M. Beasley, Ph.D., Interim Dean, Graduate Studies
Office of the Vice President for Research and Sponsored Programs
  Kofi B. Bota, Ph.D., Vice President
  Shelby Lewis, Ph.D., Associate Vice President
Office of the Vice President for Budget and Finance
  Donald R. Murphy, M.S. Vice President
  Gwendolyn Walker, M.S., Director of Human Resources
  Alvin D. Moddelmog, M.S., Director of Facilities
  Roy Bolton, M.S., Director of Administrative Servies
Office of University Development
  Charles Stephens, M.S., Vice President
  Getchel Caldwell, M.S., Associate Vice President
  William Allison, M.S., Director, Community Development Corporation
  Lucy Grigsby, M.S., LLD,. University Editor
School of Arts and Sciences

William R. Scott, Ph.D., Dean

Alexa B. Henderson, Ph.D., Associate Dean for General Education

Om P. Puri, Ph.D., Assoc.Dean for the Natural Sciences and Mathematics

Alma Vinyard, Ph.D., Associate Dean for the Humanities

School of Business Administration

    Edward Irons, DBA, Dean

    Charletta Clark, Ph.D., Associate Dean

School of Education

    Melvin R. Webb, Ph.D., Dean

    Bettye Clark, Ed. D., Associate Dean

School of Library and Information Studies

    Charles D. Churchwell, Ph.D., Dean

    Arthur Gunn, Ph.D., Associate Dean

School of Social Work

    Lou M. Beasley, Ph.D., Dean

    Richard Lyle, Ph.D., Associate Dean

Dean for Student Affairs

    Larry Earvin, Ph.D., Dean and Associate Provost

    Mary Ware, Ed.D. Associate Dean

CLARK ATLANTA UNIVERSITY FACULTY ROSTER

1990-1993

Bassam Abssulatiff, M.S., Assistant Professor, Mathematics

Saad Adnan, Ph.D., Associate Professor, Mathematics

Amos A. Ajo, Ph.D., Assistant Professor, School of Social Work

Kasim I. Ali, Ph.D., Associate Professor, School of Business

Kasim L. Alli, Ph.D., Assistant Professor, School of Business

Angelo Alonso, B. P., Asst Professor, Department of Foreign Languages

Marwam Amarin, M.S., Instructor of Physics

Hubert Ammons, B. A., Instructor, Accounting

Kofi Apenyo, Ph.D., Professor, Computer Sciences

Rosalind E. Authur, M.A., Instructor, Foreign Languages

Lillian Ashscraft-Eaton. Ph.D., Assoc. Professor, Religion and Philosophy

Mary C. Ashong, M. S. W., School of Social Work

Emmanuel V. Ashene, Ph.D., Art

Timothy Askew, M. A. English

Eerst Attah, Ph.D., SociologyM.S.W.,

Irene B. Brown, Ph.D., Associate Professor, Biology

Lorene Brown, Ph.D., Assoc. Professor, Library and Information Studies

Paul Brown, Ph.D., Assistant Professor, Foreign Languages

Paul Brown, Ph.D., Professor, Bology

William H. Brown, M.B.A., Assistant {Professor, Business Administration

John M. Browne, Ph.D., Professor, Biology

Daisy Buckner, M. S., Instructor, Mathematics

M. B. Dilla Buckner, Ed. D., English

Jeffery Caldwell, B. S., Instructor, Art

Virgil Carr, M. B. A., Assistant Professor, Business Administration

Charlie Carter, Ph.D., Associate Professor, Economics

Juanita Carter, M. S., Assistant Professor, Finance

Angela Chamble, M. A., Instructor, English

Jean Chandler-Williams, Ph.D., Assistant Professor, Psychology

Sudhanva Char, Ph.D., Assistant Professor, Economics

Huan-Ming Chang, Ph.D., Assistant Professor, Mathematics

Charles D. Churchwell, Ph.D., Library and Information Studies

Bettye Clark., Ed.D., Curriculum

Earle D. Clowney, Ph.D., Professor, Foreign Languages

Joseph Coble, Ph.D., Professor, Psychology

Thomas W. Cole, Jr., Ph.D., Professor, Chemistry

Joseph Coble, Ed. D., Associate Professor, Curriculum

Ora H. Cooks, Ed. D., Associate Professor, Curriculum

Margaret Counts-Spriggs, Ph.D., Assistant Professor, Sociology

Frank Dadzie, M. A., Instructor, Economics

Dana Dalton, M. A., Instructor Allied Health

Alex Danso, Ph.D., Assistant Professor, Public Administration

Mamie Darlington, Ph.D., School of Social Work

William Dashek, Ph.D., Associate Professor, Biology

Edward Davis, Ph.D., Professor, Decision Sciences

Jane L. Dawkins, M. A., Associate Professor Business Education

Julius Debro, Ph.D., Professor, Criminal Justice Administration

R. Benneson DeJanes, Ph.D., Professor, Political Sciences

Afrikadzata Deka, Ph.D., Visiting Professor, History

William H. Denton, Ph.D., Professor, Educational Leadership

James Devries, Ph.D., Associate Professor, English

Esmie Dias, M. A., Assistant Professor, English

David E. Dorsey, Jr., Ph.D., Professor, English

Charles F. Duncan, Ph.D., Professor, English

Myrtice Dye, Ph.D., Assist. Professor, Counseling/Human Development

K. C. Eapen, Ph.D., Associate Professor, English

Larry Earvin, Ph.D., Associate Professor, Political Science

Steven Edmond, M B.A., Assistant Professor, Finance

Henry K. Efebera, M.B.A., Assistant Professor, Accounting

Herbert Eichelberger, Ph.D., Assistant Professor, Mass Media Art

Henry Ekweani, M. A., Visiting Professor, Economics

Ralph D. Ellis, Ph.D., Associate Professor, Religion and Philosophy

Henry Elonge, Ph.D., Assistant Professor, Public Administration

Ann Fields-Ford, Ph.D., Assistant Professor, Social Work

Isabella Finkelstein, Ph.D., Professor, Biology

Robert Fishman, Ph.D., Professor, Political Science

Ahmad Flournoy, M.S., Instructor, Mathematics

Madison J. Foster II, Ph.D., Associate Professor, Social Work

Carolyn A. Fowler, Ph.D., Professor, African and African American Studies

Donna Fowler, M.S., Assistant Professor, Mass Media Arts

Lurelia Freeman, M.A., Assistant Professor, Foreign Languages

Ralph C. Frick, Ed. D., Professor, Curriculum

Hashim Garbill, Ph.D., Associate Professor, Political Science

Erseline J. Gillespie, M.A., Assistant Professor, English

Joyce Graham, Ph.D., Assistant Professor, Mass Media Arts

Rudolph Green, Ed.D., Assoc. Professor, Counseling/Human Development

Arthur Gunn, Ph.D., Professor, Library Science

Atam Gupta, Ph.D., Assistant Professor, Chemistry

Yitbarek Habte-Mariam, Ph.D., Associate Professor, Chemistry

Thomas D. Hager, M. A., Assistant Professor, Music

John E. Hall, Ph.D., Professor, Mathematics

Tarin D. Hampton, M. A., Assistant Professor, Curriculum

Carlos Handy, Ph.D., Associate Professor, Physics

Terry Harrington, M.S., Instructor, Physics

Linda Harris, M, A, Instructor, Speech Communication

Mildred Harris, M. S., Instructor, Mathematics

Winfred Harris, Ph.D., Howard Hughes Professor, Biology

Amaryllis Hawk, M. A., Assistant Professor, Speech Communication

Alexa B. Henderson, Ph.D., Professor, History

Graciela P. Hernandez, Ed. P., Assistant Foreign Languages

Christopher J. Hickey, M, F. A., Assistant Professor, Art

Elizabeth J. Higgins, Ph.D., Professor, English

Andrew O. Hill, M. A., Instructor, Management

Sylvia Hines, M. A., Instructor, Learning Resources Center

Robert A. Holmes, Ph.D., Professor, Political Science

Phillip Hood, Ed. D., Assistant Professor, Curriculum

Collete Hopkins, Ph.D., Asst. Professor, Exceptional Children
Education

M. Loretta Houston, M. S. W., Instructor, Social Work

Raymond Hughes, M. A., Assistant Professor, Curriculum

Edward Hunter, M. A., Biology

Patricia Bond Hutto, M. A., Assistant Professor, English

Edward D. Irons, D.B.A., Professor, Business Administration

Calvin Jackson, M.S., Instructor, Mathematics

Gloria James, Ph.D., Professor, Speech Communication and
Theatre Arts

Isabella T. Jenkins, Ph.D., Professor, Educational Leadership

Nathan Jideama, Ph.D., Assistant Professor, Biology

James C. Jones, M. M., Assistant Professor, Music

James T. Jones, Ph.D., Professor, Public Administration

Myrtle, Jones, M.A., Assistant Professor, Learning Resources Center

Abdulfazal Kabir, Ph.D., Asst.Professor, Library and Information Studies

Pushkar Kaul, Ph.D., Professor, Biology

Ishrat Khan, Ph.D., Assistant Professor, Chemistry

Young Hwa Kim, Ph.D., Associate Professor, Decision Sciences

Marjorie Kimbrough, M. R. Ed, Instructor, Religion and Philosophy

Linda Law, M. Ed., Instructor, History

Mohammed Latif, M.B. A., Instructor, Finance

Phyllis Lawhorn, M. A., Assistant Professor, English

Edward Leader, Ph.D., Associate Professor, Mass Media Arts

Carson Lee, D.Ed., Professor, Psychology

Carol Mitchell-Leon, M.A., Inst., Speech communication and Theater Arts

Joan A. Lewis, M.S., Associate Professor, Mass Media Arts

Shelby Lewis, Ph.D., Professor, Political Science

Janice Liddell, Ph.D., Associate Professor, English

Richard Lyle, Ph.D., Associate Professor, Social Work

Robert A. Lynn, PD., Professor, Marketing

Nina Lynn-Jenkins, M.A., Instructor, Sociology

Gretchen Maclachlan, M. S., Assistant Professor, Political Science

Robert Madison, Ph.D., Lecturer, Public Administration

Donald Martin, Ph.D., Associate Professor, Sociology

Barbara Mason, M.A., Assistant Professor, Curriculum

Henry McBay, Ph.D., Professor Emeritus, Chemistry

William McCray, M.S., Assistant Professor, Chemistry

Paul McGirt, M.A., Associate Professor, Foreign Languages

James McJunkins, M.A., Assistant Professor, Mas Media Arts

Edward McLean, Ed. D., Associate Professor, Curriculum

Negash Medhin, Ph.D., Associate Professor, Mathematics

Ronald Mickens, Ph.D., Fuller E. Callaway Professor, Physics

Stanley Mims, Ed. D., Assistant Professor, Educational Leadership

Eric Mintz, Ph.D., Associate Professor, Chemistry

Hattie Mitchell, M.S.W., Assistant Professor, Social Work

Lawrence Noble, Ph.D., Associate Professor, Political Science

Moshen Noortajalli, M.S., Assistant Professor, Computer Science

Zahra Nortajalli, M.S., Instructor, Computer Science

Lee Norris, M.A., Instructor, Mathematics

Ajamu Nyomba, Ph.D., Instructor, Economics

Donald Oehlerts, Ph.D., Assoc.Professor, Library and Information Studies

Kalu Ogbaa, Ph.D., Visiting Associate Professor, English

Olugemiga Olatidoye, M. Arch., Assistant Professor, Physics

Theda Okono, M.A., Instructor, Learning Resource Center

Stephen Ornburn, M.S., Assistant Professor, Computer Science

Osayimwense Osa, Ph.D., Visiting Associate Professor, English

James Patterson, M.M., Assistant Professor, Music

Gaylene Perrault, Ph.D., Assoc. Professor, Counseling/Human Development

Belinda Peters, M. F. A., Assistant Professor, Art

Ernestine Pickens, Ph.D., Associate Professor, English

Diane Plummer, Ph.D., Assistant Professor, Psychology

Jurella Poole, M.S. W., Associate Professor, Social Work

Robert Pritchett, M. A., Instructor, Curriculum

Om Puri, Ph.D., Garfield Merner Professor of Science, Physics

Linda Quander, Ph.D., Associate Professor, Speech Communication

Sidney Rabsatt, Ph.D., Associate Professor, Educational Leadership

Iris Rafi, M.A., Lecturer, English

Gayle Randall, M.S., Assistant Professor, Computer Science

James Reed, Ph.D., Associate Professor, Chemistry

Michael Rhodes, Ph.D., Assistant Professor, Physics

Joanne Rhone, PhD., Associate Professor, Social Work

Florence Robinson, Ph.D., Fuller E. Callaway Professor, Music

Augusto Rodriguez, Ph.D., Associate Professor, Chemistry

Julian Roebuck, Ph.D., Asst. Professor, Criminal Justice Administration

Brenda Rogers, Ph.D., Professor, Exceptional student Education

William Rogers, M. B A., Instructor, Computer Science

Michele Rubin, Ph.D., Associate Professor, Curriculum

Solomon Sears, M.S., Associate Professor, Biology

Abdulalin Shabazz, Ph.D., Professor, Mathematics

Man Sharma, Ph.D., Professor, Mathematics

Grant Shockley, Ed. D., Visiting Professor, Religion and Philosophy

Jabari Simama, Ph.D., Assistant Professor, Mass Media Arts

Sclemon Simpson, Ph.D., Associate Professor, Learning resource Center

Ranjit Singh, Ph.D., Professor, Decision Sciences

O. P. Sonha, Ph.D., Associate Professor, Physics

Frank Sisya, Ph.D., Associate Professor, Sociology

Rose Sloan, Ph.D., Associate Professor, Speech Communication

Arthur Smith, M.S., Instructor, Mathematics

Robert Smothers, Ph.D., Professor, Counseling/Human Development

Olabode Sowemimo, M. S., Instructor, Physics

Alfred Spriggs, Ph.D., Fuller E. Callaway Professor, Chemistry

Arthur Stelson, Ph.D., Associate Professor, Chemistry

Juanita Sterling, M. A. Instructor, Learning Resource Center

Juarine Stewart, Ph.D., Associate Professor, Biology

Ranga Sunkara, M.S., Assistant Professor, Allied Health

Niranjan Talukder, Ph.D., Associate Professor, Physics

Sandra Taylor, Ph.D., Associate Professor, Sociology

Roosevelt Thedford, Ph.D., Professor, Chemistry

Charles Thompson, M. S., Assistant Professor, Computer Science

Jesse Thompson, M D., Instructor, Allied Health

Margaret Thompson, M. A. Instructor, Mass Media Arts

Ruby Thompson, Ph.D., Professor, Curriculum

William Thompson, Ph.D., Professor, Physics

Lucille Tunstall, Ph.D., Professor, Allied Health

Trevor Turner, Ph.D., Associate Professor, Educational Leadership

Naomi Ward, M. S. W., Associate Professor, Social Work

Nazir Warsi, Ph.D., Professor, Computer Science

Melvin Webb, Ph.D., Professor, Science Education

L. Henry Welchel, Ph.D., Associate Professor, Religion and Philosophy

J. Ernest Wilkins, Jr., Ph.D., Distinguished Prof. of Mathematical Physics

Alex Williams, Ph.D., Robert W. Woodward Professor, Finance

Alma Williams, Ph.D., Associate Professor, History

Arthur Williams, PH.D., Associate Professor, Biology

Melvin Williams, Ph.D., Assistant Professor, Social Work

Rachel Williams, M. M., Assistant Professor, Msic

Gloria Williamson, M. Ed., Assistant Professor, Allied Health

Johnny Wilson, Ph.D., Assistant Professor, Political Science

Brenda Wright, M. A., Assistant Professor, Mass Media Arts

Verona Wynn, M. A., Assistant Professor, Mathematics

Gary Yates, M. F. A., Instructor, Speech Communication

Charleise Young, Ph.D., Assoc. Professor, English and Foreign Languages

APPENDIX II

AN HISTORICAL PERSPECTIVE ON ATLANTA UNIVERSITY CENTER COOPERATIVE RELATIONSHIPS

YEAR	ACTIVITY	COMMENTS/ SOURCE
1901	Joint Summer Session between Atlanta University and Clark College	Bacote, p. 57
1912	Atlanta University, Clark University, Morehouse, Spelman and Morris Brown Colleges and Gammon Theological Seminary Organized the Atlanta Federation of Schools for the Improvement of Negro Country Life. Ware elected president	Bacote, p. 157
1922	Discussions of merger of Atlanta University with Clark University	Brawley, p. 4
1929	Affiliation Agreement signed, forming the Atlanta University System, consisting of Atlanta University, Morehouse College and Spelman College,	Bacote, p. 268 Brawley, p. 104
1929	Joint baccalaureate services of Atlanta University, Morehouse College and Spelman College.	Bacote, p. 502
1930	General Education Board appropriation of funds to Atlanta University for purchase of land for construction of a Central library. Ground broken, 1931; building dedicated,1932.	Brawley, p. 111

1931.   General Education Board pledge
of $300,000 for construction and
equipment of Library building.
Stipulated that building shall not be
sold, conveyed, or en-cumbered by
Atlanta University prior to January 1,
1981 except on consent of 2/3 of all of
the members of the Board of Trustees
of other controlling board of Atlanta
University and 2/3 of the Boards of
Spelman and Morehouse.

1931   Agreement between Atlanta University
and Morehouse College that the
University would handle contributions
for endowment of undergraduate
work at Morehouse. Included recent
appropriation of $500,000 by the Gen.
Education Board.

1931   Agreement giving portion of land used
by Morehouse to Atlanta University
for an administration building for
Atlanta University, Morehouse College
and Spelman College.

1932   Morris Brown moved to Atlanta
University's "old" site.

1935   Morehouse College and Atlanta
University Boards of Trustees made
identical.

1936   Idea of Clark University moving close   Brawley, p. 511
to Atlanta University approved.

1938   New power plant built and equipped at
cost of $352,328 provided by General
Education Board.

1940	Atlanta University executes deed to Clark University for land directly opposite Atlanta University. Clark University moved from South Atlanta. Name changed to Clark College.	Brawley, p. 118 Bacote, p. 332
1940	Atlanta University executed deed for move- of "old" campus to Morris Brown College.	
1941	Atlanta University executes deed to Warren Church property to Clark College.	
1944	Atlanta University conveyed land to Morris Brown for sum of $1, with reversionary clause.	
1945	Atlanta University conveyed property to Spelman College.	
1953	Study by Management Consultants: Cresap, McCormick, and Paget.	
1954	Atlanta University System of free student exchange for certain courses.	Brawley, p. 9
1956	Revised Contract for Affiliation approved. Created AUCenter with all institutions equal member	Brawley, p. 143
1957	Interdenominational Theological Center established, replacing Gammon as the sixth institution in the AU Center	Bacote, p. 397
1962	Cooperative fund-raising effort by the four undergraduate colleges to raise $500,000 in Atlanta.	Brawley, p. 241
1964	Establishment of the Atlanta University Center Office of Exec. Sec. created.	
1968	Atlanta University gives deed in fee simple to land at the southeast corner of Fair and Chestnut Streets to Clark College	

1973   Reorganization of Atlanta University Center AUC, Inc. Replaced AUCC; Chancellor created.

1977   Joint Resolution supporting Center Library; Signed by all presidents

1978   Report of Special Study Committee on AUC, Inc.

1987   Resolutions by Clark College and Atlanta University Boards of Trustees to explore opportunities for increased collaboration, including merger. Consolidation of Clark College and Atlanta University approved.

APPENDIX III

CLARK ATLANTA UNIVERSITY, INC.

Financial Statement Comparison of Current Funds Revenues, Expenditures, and Other Changes for Years Ending June 30, 1989 and June 30, 1994

	1989	1994
REVENUES:		
Tuition and Fees	$15,675	$36,472
Government grants/contracts	12,192	54,642
Private gifts and grants	7,433	11,266
State and local grants—		1,101
Endowment Income	861	673
Sales, auxiliary enterprises	3,067	5,421
Other sources	773	377
Total revenues	40,002	109,952

EXPENSES AND MANDATORY TRANSFERS:		
Education and General		
Instruction	9,413	28,227
Research	1,473	15,707
Public Service	1,576	14,796
Academic support	3,025	5,764
Student services	1,728	5,919
Operation/maintenance of plant	2,995	8,343
Student aid 5,736	15,683	
Institutional support	10,752	10,946
Educational and general expenses	36,699	105,385
Mandatory transfers	138	398

Total educational and general	36,837	105,783
Auxiliary enterprises	2,651	4,007
Total expenses	39,487	109,790
OTHER TRANSFERS	626	2,915
NET INCREASE IN ASSETS	$1,141	$3,077

In June 1993, the Financial Accounting Standards Board issued Statements of Financial Accounting Standards Nos. 116 and 117, which Clark Atlanta University was required to adopt. In 1995, the University adopted FAS 116; in 1996, FAS 117, which make comparisons of financial statements after 1994 with prior years more difficult than a year-to-year comparison. The differences are especially pronounced in the recording of tuition and fee revenue, private gifts and grants revenue, and expenditures for student financial aid. In the following areas, however, direct comparisons can be made:

APPENDIX IV

Growth over first ten-year period
Clark Atlanta University

Category	09/89	1998
Enrollment (HCT)	3,151	5,800
First-Year Applications	2,300	>7,000
Degrees Awarded	625	1,005
Teaching Faculty	183	330
Physical Space (Sq. ft., 000)	338	680
Student Housing Spaces	1,140	1,900
Parking Spaces	710	1,540
Financial ($ in million)		
Total Operating Budget	40	122
Endowment	17	32
Private Gifts/Grants	7	12
Federal Grants/Contracts	12	42
Total Assets	63	196

Since 1988, the SAT scores or entering freshmen increased 150 points and just over $570 million had been invested in the University to support academic programs, research and public service activities, infrastructure enhancements, and new and renovated facilities. Of this amount, almost $150 million were applied to new construction and renovated facilities from the following three sources ($ in million):

Facility	Fed	Priv	Bonds	Tot
Research Center		$27.0	9.0	$36.0
Sage-Bacote Hall		5.0		5.0
Ware/Bumstead Halls	2.5		3.0	5.5
Beckwith Dorm			5.0	5.0
Brawley Hall	0.5			0.5
Annex H	0.1	0.1		0.2
Oglethorpe Hall	1.0			1.0
Haven-Warren Hall	1.0	0.25		1.25
Knowles Hall	1.0			1.0
Trevor Arnett Hall		0.5		0.5
Art Gallery	2.0	0.5		2.5
Consolidation Activities		1.1		1.1
Campus Wiring/YK2	0.5	2.0		2.5
BANNER	2.0			2.0
Distance Learning	1.0	1.5		2.5
Res. Apts.			17.0	17.0
Football Stadium		12.0		12.0
Dorm AC		1.0		1.0
Simon Courts		1.0	2.0	3.0
Park Street Church		1.0		1.0
Tennis Courts		0.1		0.1
Biology Bldg.	2.5	2.5		5.0
Student Center			5.0	5.0
Parking Deck			3.0	3.0
Paschal Center			4.0	4.0
Land Acquisitions		1.5	1.7	3.2
Demo/Simon Courts		0.2		0.2
Promenade		3.0		3.0
LL Centers	1.0			1.0
Heritage Commons			17.0	17.0

New Academic Center	7.0		7.0
Totals	$46.6	$44.75	57.7	149.05

In addition to the private gifts ($15.1 million) made possible through the 1996 Olympics and grants from the State of Georgia through the Georgia Research Alliance ($8.0 million), funds were raised from the private sector including, as part of the Second Capital Campaign, $7 million raised from the Woodruff and J. Bulow Campbell Foundations and several smaller donors prior to 2002 that served as the basic financing for a new academic center. The other major sources of private funds were The United Methodist Church, and the Woodruff, J. Bulow Campbell, Kresge, Ford, Mott, Lily, Kellogg and Knight Foundations. Annual alumni giving increased to more than $700,000.

APPENDIX V

Honorary Degrees Conferred
(May 1988 through May 2002)

Atlanta University   Clark College
May 1988   May 1988
Wyche Fowler, LL.D.   Vernon Jordan, Jr., LL.D.
Willie Lewis Brown, Jr., LL.D.   Jessie L. Jackson, D.D.
                                            Dorothy E. Branson, LL.D.

October 1988: Charter Day
   Lucy Clemmons Grigsby, Litt.D.
   William Gray, L.L.D.

May 1989: First Consolidated Commencement
   Anne Cox Chambers, LL.D. (AU)
   Lou Rawls, L.H.D. (one from AU; one from CC)
   Reatha Clark King, LL.D. (CC)
   Colin Luther Powell, LL.D. (AU)
   Carl Ware, LL.D. (CC)

July 1989
   Atty. Donald Hollowell, LL.D. (CC)

May 1990
   Clifton Wharton, Jr., LL.D.

June 1990
   Nelson Rolihlala Mandela, LL.D.

May 1991
   Lionel Hampton, L.H.D.
   John Lewis, LL.D.
   Herbert Miller, LL.D.

July 1991
   Alhaji Hassan Adamu, LL.D.
   William B. McClean, D.D.

February 1992
   Desmond Mpilo Tutu, D.D.

May 1992
   Leon Howard Sullivan, LL.D.

October 1992
   Babicar Ndiaye, LL.D.

February 1993
   Quincy Jones, L.H.D.
   William Warfield, L.H.D.

May 1993
   John Henrik Clarke, Litt.D.
   Henry Anderson Pfiffner, LL.D.

March 1994
Donald R. Keough, LL.D.
Bryant C. Gumbel, L.H.D.

May 1994
Clarence Cooper, LL.D.
Hardy R. Franklin, Litt.D.

May 1995
E. J. Josey, Litt.D.

May 1996
John H. Johnson, H.H.D.

May 1997
Margaret Blake Roach, LL.D.
Phylicia Rashad, L.H.D.

May 1998
Ronald Dellums, LL.D.

May 1999
David Satcher, LL.D.

May 2000
Henry L. (Hank) Aaron, LL.D.
Xernona Clayton, Litt.D.
James S. Thomas, D.D.

May 2001

 William H. Gray III, LL.D. (CAU hood)

 Wynton Marsalis, L.H.D.

May 2002

 Walter Kimbrough, L.H.D.

 Joyce F. Brown, L.H.D.

 H. Carl McCall, LL.D.

 Cecily Tyson, Litt.D. (CAU Hood)

Secretary of State
Business Services and Regulation
Suite 306, West Tower
2 Martin Luther King Jr. Dr.
Atlanta, Georgia 30334

APPENDIX VI

```
CHARTER NUMBER    : 8812635 DN
COUNTY            : FULTON
DATE INCORPORATED : 07/01/88
EXAMINER          : STACY GILLEY
TELEPHONE         : 404/656-2821
```

REQUESTED BY:

PATRISE M. PERKINS-HOOKER
132 MITCHELL ST SW, 3RD FL
ATLANTA GA 30303

CERTIFICATE OF INCORPORATION

I, MAX CLELAND, Secretary of State and the Corporations Commissioner of the State of Georgia do hereby certify, under the seal of my office, that

"CLARK ATLANTA UNIVERSITY, INC."

has been duly incorporated under the laws of the State of Georgia on the date set forth above, by the filing of articles of incorporation in the office of the Secretary of State and the fees therefore paid, as provided by law, and that attached hereto is a true copy of said articles of incorporation.

WITNESS, my hand and official seal, in the City of Atlanta and the State of Georgia on the date set forth below.

DATE: JULY 11, 1988

MAX CLELAND
SECRETARY OF STATE

H. WAYNE HOWELL
DEPUTY SECRETARY OF STATE

SECURITIES   CEMETERIES   CORPORATIONS   CORPORATIONS HOT-LINE
656-2894   656-3079   656-2817   404-656-2222
                                                        Outside Metro-Atlanta

168

ARTICLES OF INCORPORATION

OF

CLARK ATLANTA UNIVERSITY

1.

The name of the corporation shall be:

Clark Atlanta University.

This corporation shall be a nonprofit corporation organized and operated under the "Georgia Nonprofit Corporation Code."

2.

The term for which this corporation shall have existence shall be perpetual.

3.

The purpose of the corporation is to create and maintain a successor institution of higher learning to Clark College and Atlanta University, offering instruction and granting degrees in such courses of study and in such curricula, and sponsoring and undertaking such research and studies as the Board of Trustees shall determine are in the best interests of the institution. The Board of Trustees, upon recommendation of the faculty department of study from which a degree is to be conferred, shall have power to confer such degrees as now or may hereafter be conferred by institutions of like character on such persons as the Board of Trustees may deem to be entitled thereto. The corporation may undertake such other projects and activities

-1-

169

as the Board of Trustees shall determine to be in furtherance of aforesaid educational purposes.

4.

The corporation shall have no capital stock and no members, and shall not be conducted for pecuniary gain or profit to anyone; rather its purpose shall be to give, promote and extend instruction and education in the arts, sciences, professions, and to encourage and promote research and study in all branches of learning.

5.

The corporation shall be managed, and its affairs conducted and powers exercised by a Board of Trustees, which shall consist of not less than forty (40) nor more than forty-nine (49) members. The number and method of election and clasification of Trustees shall be as provided in the By-Laws of the corporation.

The names and addresses of the persons who are the initial Trustees of the corporation are as follows:

Name	Address
Charles Ackerman	10040 Crown Point Parkway Atlanta, Georgia 30338
Dr. Delores P. Aldridge	2931 Yucca Drive Decatur, Georgia 30032
Marvin S. Arrington	132 Mitchell Street, S.W. Third Floor Atlanta, Georgia 30303

-2-

170

Dwight Gary Calhoun	146 Mildred Street, Apt. B
	Atlanta, Georgia 30314
Dr. Clarence Coleman	779½ Martin Luther King Dr.
	Atlanta, Georgia 30314
Bishop Ernest A. Fitzgerald	The United Methodist Church Atlanta Area 159 Ralph McGill Boulevard, N.E. Atlanta, Georgia 30365
Donald Fletcher	One Waterway Court
	Rockville, Maryland 20853
Lamond Godwin	First Vice President American Express Bank, Ltd. World Financial Center New York, New York 10285-2150
Mel Gregory	The Equitable Financial Companies 9000 Central Park West, Suite 800 Atlanta, Georgia 30328
Paul Hatchett	2791 Handy Drive, N.W.
	Atlanta, Georgia 30318
Dr. Cornelius L. Henderson	The United Methodist Church 159 Ralph McGill Boulevard, N.E. Atlanta, Georgia 30365
Hylan T. Hubbard, III	Aetna Life and Casualty Company 151 Farmington Avenue, D-111 Hartford, Connecticut 06156
Dr. Major J. Jones	111 James P. Brawley Drive, S.W.
	Atlanta, Georgia 30314
James R. Kuse	President - Georgia Gulf P.O. Box 105197 Atlanta, Georgia 30348
Dr. Carson Lee	775 Lynn Circle, S.W.
	Atlanta, Georgia 30311

Dr. Elridge W. McMillan	- Southern Education Foundation 340 W. Peachtreet, N.W. Suite 250 Atlanta, Georgia 30308
Mrs. Margaret Roach	1651 N.W. 26th Street
	Fort Lauderdale, Florida 33311
Bishop James S. Thomas	The United Methodist Church P.O. Box 2800 North Canton, Ohio 44720
Carl Ware	The Coca-Cola Company Post Office Drawer 1734 Atlanta, Georgia 30301
Welcom H. Watson	United Federal Building 3600 North Federal Building Fort Lauderdale, Florida 33339
Cecil Alexander -	524 W. Peachtree Street
	Atlanta, Georgia 30308
Kofi Bota	223 James P. Brawley Drive
	Atlanta, Georgia 30314
Raphael Boyd	223 James P. Brawley Drive
	Atlanta, Georgia 30314
Thomas O. Cordy	463 Plum Street
	Atlanta, Georgia 30311
Lawrence R. Cowart	310 North Avenue P.O. Drawer 1734 Atlanta, Georgia 30312
Myrtle Davis	100 Edgewood Avenue, Room 313
	Atlanta, Georgia 30303
Robert Davis	2249 Larchwood Road
	Atlanta, Georgia 30310

-4-

172

Dr. Harold E. Doley, Jr.	- 616 Paronne Street
	New Orleans, Louisiana 70113
Hon. Jack P. Etheridge	Emory University Law School
	Atlanta, Georgia 30322
Michael R. Hollis	Grant Building
	Atlanta, Georgia 30303
Gerald T. Horton	University of Georgia
	Management Department
	Athens, Georgia 30602
Dr. Morris F. X. Jeff, Jr.	1300 Pardido Street
	Room 1W1C City Hall
	New Orleans, Louisiana 70112
Dwight C. Minton	469 North Harrison Street
	Princeton, New Jersey 08540
Dr. James Palmer	970 Martin Luther King Jr. Drive
	Atlanta, Georgia 30314
George R. Puskar	3414 Peachtree Road
	Atlanta, Georgia 30326-1162
Sidney Topol	1 Technology Parkway
	P.O. Box 105600
	Atlanta, Georgia 30348
Prentiss Q. Yancey, Jr, Esq.	2400 1st National Bank Towers
	Atlanta, Georgia 30383
Senator Sam Nunn	3241 Dirksen Building
	Washington, D.C. 20510

-5-

173

INDEX

CPSIA information can be obtained at www.ICGtesting.com
Printed in the USA
LVOW11*0835280216

477017LV00001B/1/P